Bible of the Oppressed

JOHN E. COCKAYNE, JR.

Bible
of the Oppressed

ELSA TAMEZ

Translated from the Spanish by
Matthew J. O'Connell

ORBIS BOOKS

Maryknoll, New York 10545

The Catholic Foreign Mission Society of America (Maryknoll) recruits and trains people for overseas missionary service. Through Orbis Books Maryknoll aims to foster the international dialogue that is essential to mission. The books published, however, reflect the opinions of their authors and are not meant to represent the official position of the society.

Chapters 1 through 5 of this translation were originally published as *La Biblia de los oprimidos: La opresión en la teología bíblica* by Departamento Ecuménico de Investigaciones, Apdo. 339, S. Pedro Montes de Oca, San José, Costa Rica, copyright © 1979 by Elsa Tamez; Chapters 6 and 7 are taken from *La hora de la vida,* also published by DEI, copyright © 1978 by Elsa Tamez. The original Spanish versions have been slightly revised for the English translation.

Unless otherwise indicated, quotations from Scripture are from the *Revised Standard Version.*

Library of Congress Cataloging in Publication Data

Tamez, Elsa.
  Bible of the oppressed.

  Translation of: La Biblia de los oprimidos and portions of La hora de la vida.
  Includes bibliographical references and index.
  1. Sociology, Biblical. 2. Jews—Politics and government—to A.D. 70. 3. Social conflict in the Bible. 4. Liberation theology. I. Tamez, Elsa. Hora de la vida. English. Selections. 1982. II. Title.
BS670.T2613   261.8'3456   81-18797
ISBN 0-88344-035-0 (pbk.)   AACR2

Contents

Abbreviations

BAC   *Biblioteca de autores cristianos* (Madrid: Editorial Católica)

JB   *Jerusalem Bible*

NEB   *The New English Bible*

RSV   *Revised Standard Version*

TDNT *Theological Dictionary of the New Testament,* ed. G. Kittel, trans. G. Bromiley (Grand Rapids: Eerdmans, 1964-74)

PART I

OPPRESSION IN THE OLD TESTAMENT

My intention in Part I is to study the experience of oppression as recorded in the Old Testament. This means determining why oppression occurs; who the oppressors are and who the oppressed are; what the characteristic traits of each of these two groups are; what the methods are that the oppressors use; and what forms oppression takes.[1]

The story told in the various biblical accounts is one of oppression and struggle, as is the history of our Latin American peoples. In fact, our present story can be seen as a continuation of what we are told in biblical revelation. For this reason, I think that reflection on oppression and liberation in the Scriptures is not to be regarded simply as a study of one more biblical theme. Rather oppression and liberation are the very substance of the entire historical context within which divine revelation unfolds, and only by reference to this central fact can we understand the meaning of faith, grace, love, peace, sin, and salvation.

God's self-revelation occurs in the context of a history of conflict; it is also clear that in this history God is on the side of the subjugated. This experience of God, which runs through the whole Bible, finds expression today in the religious life of oppressed peoples who are seeking their liberation. To take but one example, the Mass of the Nicaraguan Farmers is filled from beginning to end with this same experience. Consider how the prayer in the Kyrie chant repeats that of many of the psalms:

Christ, Christ Jesus,
be one with us.
Lord, Lord my God,
be one with us.
Christ, Christ Jesus,
take sides
not with the *oppressor class*
that squeezes dry and devours
the community,
but with the *oppressed,*
with my people
thirsting for peace.

And the final section of the Creed, when interpreted from the viewpoint of the oppressed, proves to be a wise summation of the central gospel message:

I believe in you,
my companion,
the human Christ, the worker Christ,
the conqueror of death.
By your measureless sacrifice
you have begotten the *new human being*
who is destined for *liberation.*
You are living
in every arm raised
to defend the people
against exploitative domination;
because you are alive on the ranch,
in the factory, in the school
I believe in your truceless struggle,
I believe in your *resurrection.*

When we Christians speak of oppression in Latin America, we cannot afford to do it in abstract, universal, nonanalytic terms. We are speaking, after all, of an experience that is very concrete: of political and economic tyranny, of despoliation, torture, assassination, imprisonment, disappearance, all against the backdrop of a fetishized structure with a deadly logic of its own.[2] It is a logic that leads to the denial of all the basic rights of the human person and of downtrodden peoples. We must also bear in mind the methods and motives of oppression, the constant changes in the style of tyranny, the increasingly threatening presence of transnational corporations, and the ideologies of National Security and limited democracy that have for their purpose the preservation of the capitalist system and its oppressive structure.[3]

The same can be said of the biblical experience of oppression. When the Bible speaks of oppression, it does not have in mind primarily a soul in torment or afflicted by "unidentified spirits." The language of the Bible is always very concrete. As my analysis will show, in biblical theology "oppression" refers to a real experience that is directly related to agents of oppression and to the logic which leads the rich to augment their possessions at whatever cost. The oppressed and the poor suffer exploitation and death, both physical and psychological; they suffer discrimination and degradation. To speak of liberation, therefore, is to speak of the struggle of an oppressed people in quest of their rights and spurred on by the hope that the victory will be real because their God is at their side in the struggle.

For the Bible oppression is the basic cause of poverty, but I want also to introduce a middle term that sheds some light: despoliation, or theft. In other words, the oppressor steals from the oppressed and impoverishes them. The oppressed are therefore *those who have been impoverished,* for while the oppressor oppresses the poor because they are poor and powerless, the poor have become poor in the first place because they have been oppressed. The principal motive for oppression is the eagerness to pile up wealth, and this desire is connected with the fact that the oppressor is an idolater.

A fortunate historical event occurred while I was working on this study: the successful revolution of the Nicaraguan people, in

July of 1979. It is an event that will be kept in the hearts of all the oppressed, a glimpse of the satisfaction of an exploited people's longing for freedom. The struggle of the people of Nicaragua and of their leaders, the Sandinista National Liberation Front, is a form of witness that raises the hopes of the oppressed majority among the Latin American peoples. It tells them: the power of the oppressor is not everlasting; the oppressed who struggle will attain their liberation.

The participation of Christians in the whole process of liberation in Latin America and especially in the Nicaraguan revolution has no precedent. Their present involvement therefore constitutes what Gustavo Gutiérrez calls "the major event in the life of the Christian community."[4] This means that in Nicaragua, for example, militant Christians among the Sandinistas and among the people generally are experiencing and celebrating their faith in a different way. For them, the rejection of and the struggle against an oppressive system is not simply a matter of politics but a question of faith as well; for them, the liberation of the oppressed is God's own cause (Ps. 74:22; Ps. 72:12–14).

This praxis of liberation has given rise to new approaches to the interpretation of the Bible. It is precisely in this context that I shall be attempting in my study to make a few basic contributions to biblical-theological thought. In doing so, I shall be emphasizing the "historical recovery of the biblical message, its liberation from all universal, ahistorical abstractions and all timeless concepts."[5]

There is an almost complete absence of the theme of oppression in European and North American biblical theology. But the absence is not surprising, since it is possible to tackle this theme only within an existential situation of oppression. As a result, the theology of liberation, which came into existence in Latin America, regards this historical experience of oppression and liberation as the root of all its theological work. In this study, therefore, the reader should not expect to find a separate section on "the state of the question" with regard to a biblical analysis of the experience of oppression.

In my study I have preferred to look at the Old Testament as a whole. I shall not be focusing my attention on a single book. My aim, rather, is to ascertain what the experience of oppression is *in the theology of the Bible.* Although I do not include the New Testament, I hope to provide guidelines for later New Testament study, by reason of the continuity between the Old Testament and the New in the questions with which I am dealing.

I am aware of the difficulties entailed in this approach to the reading of the Bible: the passage of time between one situation and another, the diversity of authors and their ideologies, the questions relating to documentary sources, the changes in the Hebrew language through the course of time, the differences between literary genres, foreign influences. Yet I accept the risks involved, because, if we are to be realistic, it is almost impossible in a book like the Bible to analyze a theme such as mine in a scientifically rigorous way. To relate redaction history with the sociopolitical and economic situation from the viewpoint solely of oppression would be an extremely difficult undertaking, and would in the end result, however scientific the method used, only in uncertainties. Our Bible, God's word, has undergone what any text that originates in human history undergoes—corruption, unintelligibility, corrections, omissions, interpolations, juxtapositions, anachronisms, repetitions, and so on.

Consequently, taking into account the tools of analysis that are available to me, as well as my own abilities, I have chosen the following approach:

1. In Chapters 1 and 2, I consider almost all the passages in which one of the nine Hebrew roots meaning "oppression" appears.[6]

2. By looking at each root in all the contexts in which it appears, I have endeavored to move beyond the roots' etymological meaning and to determine the connotations it acquires from its contextual uses. I have taken into account the structure of the passage, noted the terms or specific situations relating to each root, and noted the frequency of use (note, for example, the constant use of *gazal,* "despoliation," in combination with the various roots meaning "oppression"; the same can be said of other terms, such as "poor," "violence," "rich," "injustice," "cry").

With the help of these and other factors that will become clear as the work proceeds, I have highlighted the nuances of meaning in each of the Hebrew roots, thus uncovering the meaning of the experience of oppression. Throughout the work I have consulted Hebrew lexicons and concordances as well as scriptural commentaries.

3. In Chapters 3 and 4, I look once again at the structure of the passages in which the Hebrew roots I have analyzed appear, and I examine in detail: *(a)* the agents and objects of oppression; *(b)* the underlying causes of oppression; *(c)* the methods used in order to oppress. I also examine certain texts in which no direct use is made of any of the Hebrew roots I have analyzed, but which nonetheless describe a situation of oppression (e.g., 1 Kings 21).

In organizing the data I have distinguished two important levels or areas: *(a)* oppression of one nation by another; and *(b)* oppression within a nation itself.

In regard to the first level, I begin with a special reference to the oppression of the Hebrews in Egypt. I proceed in this way not only because of the importance of this particular historical context but also because the story is a more coherent one than others, and the events making it up are presented in a clearer sequence.

In dealing with the second level, I focus attention chiefly upon oppression in Israel and Judah during the age of the prophets (Amos, Isaiah, Zephaniah, Jeremiah, Ezekiel).

NOTES

1. Tomás Hanks' essay "La opresión y la pobreza en la teología bíblica" (Oppression and Poverty in Biblical Theology) was an inspiration for this study and a great help in carrying it out. I have however endeavored to go into the problem more fully, to treat certain aspects in greater detail, and, in general, to move a step further in the investigation initiated by Hanks. My analysis, then, especially in Chapters 1 and 2, reflects what is said in his article, but adds new contributions and approaches to the subject.

Hanks has been a professor of Old Testament at the Seminario Bíblico Latinoamericano since 1965. The paper to which I refer was published in *Estudios Ecuménicos,* 32/78 (Mexico City, CEE), and in DOCET, series G, no. 8 (Lima, Celadec). In a revised and expanded form the essay will appear as a book entitled *Opresión, pobreza y liberación. Reflexiones bíblicas* (Miami: Caribe, forthcoming) with an English translation to be published by Orbis Books.

2. See Franz Hinkelammert's discussion of the fetishization of economic relations in his book *Las armas ideológicas de la muerte* (San José: Educa,

1977), and his article "Las raíces económicas de la idolatría: la metafísica del empresario," in *La lucha de los dioses: Los ídolos de la opresión y la búsqueda del Dios Liberador* (San José, Costa Rica: Departamento Ecuménico de Investigaciones; Managua, Nicaragua: Centro Antonio Valdivieso, 1980), to be published as *The Battle of the Gods* by Orbis Books.

3. See especially the contributions of the Departamento Ecuménico de Investigaciones (DEI) in its books: Hugo Assmann, ed., *Carter y la lógica del Imperialismo,* 2 vols. (San José: Educa, 1978); E. Tamez and S. Trinidad, eds., *Capitalismo: Violencia y antivida,* 2 vols. (San José: Educa, 1978); Xabier Gorostiga, ed., *Para entender América Latina* (San José: Educa, 1979).

4. Gustavo Gutiérrez, "Teología desde el reverso de la historia" in *La fuerza histórica de los pobres* (Lima: CEP, 1979), p. 305; English translation to be published by Orbis Books.

5. Victorio Araya, *Lectura política de la Biblia: Antología* (San José: PRODIADIS, 1979), p. 2.

6. See Hanks, "La opresión y la pobreza en la teología bíblica."

Chapter 1

Oppression at the International Level

Let me summarize what we can learn from an analysis of certain Hebrew words in their contexts:

1. The experience of oppression is closely connected with the antagonism that exists between rich and poor, whether these be whole nations or sectors within nations.
2. The experience of oppression involves:
   a. *'anah:* the degradation of the human person; oppression affects the inmost being of the person (see also *daka'*); the tyranny of the powerful; the sexual violation of woman;
   b. *'ashaq:* the violent despoliation and consequently the impoverishment of the oppressed; ruthless violence; injustice;
   c. *lahats:* the smashing blow of the oppressor and the immediate outcry of the oppressed;
   d. *nagash:* violent exploitation, chiefly by means of forced labor; compulsion to produce; pressure from the oppressor;
   e. *yanah:* deadly violence used for the despoliation of the poor; exploitation in the form of enslavement; fraud;
   f. *ratsats:* the crushing and despoiling of the poor;

   g. *daka':* the grinding effect of oppression that penetrates the
      whole person, oppressing interiorly as well as exteriorly; a
      knocking down;
      (the oppressor will experience the same in turn);
   h. *dak:* the vexation of the poor, and the persistent hope of
      the poor for the establishment of a new and just order;
   i. *tok:* the tyranny of the oppressor, exercised in deceit.
3. The underlying cause of oppression is the desire to pile up
   riches; this explains the repeated appearance of despoliation
   and theft.

When the Hebrew texts speak to us of oppression, oppressors,
and the oppressed, they use sixteen different lexemes, or roots,
each of which can take the form of verbs, nouns, or adjectives. I
shall analyze nine of these sixteen roots—the ones I consider
more important. All of them basically convey the idea of oppression.[1] In alphabetical order the nine are: *daka', dakak, yanah,
lahats, nagash, 'anah, 'ashaq, ratsats,* and *takak.*

The set of words used to mean "oppression" in the international context are *nagash, 'anah,* and *lahats.*

1. The oppressor exerts pressure on the oppressed (nagash)[2]

The root *nagash* means "to oppress, exploit, force, exert pressure." When the lexeme takes the form of a substantive, it means
"oppressor, tyrant." In the context of the Exodus, English
translations usually render this noun as "taskmaster" or "slave-
driver" (Exod. 5:6, 10,14).

It is quite probable that the Ugaritic root meaning "over-
whelm with work" is related to the Hebrew *nagash.*[3] The early
Elohist chapters of the Book of Exodus speak of the excessive
amount of work the Hebrews had to do for the benefit of the
Egyptians. The Egyptians "made their lives bitter with hard
service, in mortar and brick, and in all kinds of work in the
field; in all their work they made them serve with rigor" (Exod.
1:14). "The taskmasters [*nagash*] were urgent, saying, 'Complete your work, your daily task, as when there was straw' "
(Exod. 5:13).

The oppressors *(nagash),* then, exerted a cruel and dehumanizing pressure on the Hebrews.

Referring to Job 39:7 where the term *nagash* occurs, Hanks comments: "Such texts suggest that when people suffer oppression, they lose their human dignity and are reduced to an animal existence. Instead of enjoying the freedom that God intended for them as God's image bearers (Gen. 1:27, 28), others lord it over them."[4]

If we advert to the contexts in which this Hebrew root appears in the Old Testament, certain important connotations of the word become clear.

Among the variety of meanings this word can have are the two interrelated concepts of "oppression" and "bringing pressure to bear." The oppressors are anxious to lay hold of the product of their exploitation. That is to say, there is a degree of pressure exerted by the exploiter on the exploited. The product yielded by the exploitative pressure must become available quickly; it is urgently needed. Thus in Egypt, for example, the "overseers" *(nagash)* use violence to force the Hebrews to work: the cities must be built quickly, and therefore a larger number of bricks is needed daily (Exod. 5:6–17). In Isaiah 58:3 we find a similar idea: a connotation of anxiety and greed. The oppressors are concerned about their own business and are constantly exploiting the workers, as they are pressured to produce more quickly.

Conversely, the very action of bringing pressure to bear on others and requiring onerous toil of them connotes oppressive activity. We observe this in 2 Kings 23:35. Centuries after the events of the Exodus, Pharaoh Neco of Egypt laid a tribute on the people of Judah. King Jehoiakim, in turn, had to levy taxes on the citizenry. Jehoiakim pressured/oppressed *(nagash)* his people to make them supply the tribute money. Here the domination/pressuring and oppression/pressure connections are quite clear.

Deuteronomy 15:2, 3 refers to the sabbatical year.[5] The law of the sabbatical year was intended to protect persons who had borrowed with a pledge to repay, but whose debt was heavy in comparison with their real resources. According to the law, no pressure was to be brought to bear, no steps taken to exact payment of the debt, for this would be oppression.

Now the nature of the remission is this: every creditor who holds the person of his neighbour in bond must grant him remission; he may not exact payment [*nagash:* bring pressure/oppress] from his fellow or his brother once the latter appeals to Yahweh for remission [Deut. 15:2 JB].[6]

It would sometimes happen in Israel that in order to pay a debt poor people would sell a son into slavery or, lacking this possibility, the father would work to pay off the debt.[7]

The connection between "oppress" and "bring pressure" can also be seen in Isaiah 3:5, where different versions disagree in translating the niphal form *nogesh*.[8]

When the prophet Zechariah speaks of the new earth, he says that Yahweh will guard the land and "no oppressor *[nagash]* shall again overrun them" (Zech. 9:8). In other words, there will be no more oppression; there will be freedom and relief from all oppression.

In summary, oppression *(nagash)* means that the oppressed are (1) *exploited:* someone is trying to profit through their dehumanization, and (2) *afflicted:* they live in a permanent state of anxiety as they carry out the orders of the oppressor.

2. Oppression degrades the poor *('anah)*[9]

The word *'anah* means: "to oppress, exploit; humiliate, degrade; subdue (or subject), dominate; afflict, distress; force or violate (a woman); fast (almost always with the word *nephesh*)."[10]

The situation of Israel had been foretold in Genesis 15:13: "Know of a surety that your descendants will be sojourners in a land that is not theirs, and will be slaves there, and they will be oppressed [*'anah*] for four hundred years." That is just what happened: "They set taskmasters over them to afflict *('anah)* them with heavy burdens" (Exod. 1:11).

Afterwards, when the oppressed people had obtained their freedom, they would always remember that time. Indeed, their creed would forever record the oppressive and degrading situation that had been theirs in Egypt and their experience of their struggle against domination: "And the Egyptians treated us

harshly, and afflicted [*'anah*] us, and laid upon us hard bondage" (Deut. 26:6).

This was a people that suffered brutal oppression and repression. The oppression the Hebrews suffered in body extended as
well to the innermost parts of their being.[11] It touched their inner
selves, the transcendental part of their being, their dignity, their
persons. It represented a degradation of the human being, a
seizure as it were of the divine image in the person. The Koehler-
Baumgartner lexicon attributes to *'anah* the meaning not only of
"oppress" but also of "make someone feel dependent."[12] To
experience dependence in this way is degrading to the person.

This is to say that oppression or exploitation *('anah)* is accompanied by human degradation and humiliation. It is precisely
this oppression reaching to the innermost self that moves the
God of the Hebrews: "I have seen the affliction [oppression/
degradation: *'anah*] of my people who are in Egypt and have
heard their cry because of their taskmasters [*nagash*]; I know
their sufferings" (Exod. 3:7).

If we analyze the Old Testament texts in which the term *'anah*
occurs we often find implied the imposition of another's will.[13]
In other words, the oppressed subject is forced to submit. Oppression is not something that happens due to the play of natural
forces in the world; there are agents who cause it. The clearest
example of this imposition of will is the use of *'anah* for the
violation of a woman.[14] These actions not only humiliate a person (in Israelite morality, to violate a woman was to disgrace
her); they also represent the imposition of a stronger party's will.
" 'No, my brother, do not force [*'anah*] me; for such a thing is
not done in Israel; do not do this wanton folly.'" . . . But he
would not listen to her; and being stronger than she, he forced
[*'anah*] her and lay with her" (2 Sam. 13:12, 14).

Neither during the Egyptian oppression nor in any other situation recorded in the Bible did individuals voluntarily undergo
humiliation, degradation, and oppression.

The only instance of voluntary "humiliation" *('anah)* is when
one "submits," "yields," "agrees with and obediently follows"
God or God's commandments.[15]

These two shades of meaning (degrade/force to yield) may be
seen in two verses of Psalm 119. "I am sorely afflicted [humili-

ated, degraded: *'anah*]; give me life, O Lord, according to thy word!" (Ps. 119:107). Here the oppression/degradation precedes the promise of life. Another text shows a different shade of meaning: "I know, O Lord, that thy judgments are right, and that in faithfulness thou hast afflicted me [forced me to yield: *'anah*]" (Ps. 119:75).

The oppressed never voluntarily humble themselves *('anah)* before the oppressor. The oppressor actively oppresses, exploits, humiliates. On the other hand, we note that oppressors never humble themselves (give in) before God. Yahweh says as much to Pharaoh, who is oppressing the Israelites: "How long will you refuse to humble yourself [yield, submit: *'anah*] before me? Let my people go, that they may serve me" (Exod. 10:3). Yahweh is saying here: "Submit to me and act justly: set my enslaved people free." Submission to God entails leaving the paths of oppression and following the paths of justice.

Oppressors cannot submit to God because their state does not allow it. If they do seem to "submit," they simply are being radically inconsistent with themselves; they are inauthentic. God rejects this absolutely.

Oppressors cry out to Yahweh: "Why have we fasted [*tsum*], and thou seest it not? Why have we humbled ourselves [*'anah nephesh*], and thou takest no knowledge of it?" But Yahweh answers them: "Behold, you fast only to quarrel and to fight and to hit with wicked fist. Fasting like yours this day will not make your voice to be heard on high" (Isa. 58:3, 4).

In a number of texts the verb *'anah* has God for its active subject: God oppresses, forces into submission, humbles, disgraces. But in these instances the objects or direct complements of the verbs—i.e., the ones oppressed—are quite different from those ordinarily called "oppressed."

In principle, God is not an oppressor of his people (Job 37:23). However, in order to secure equity and justice *(rob, tsedeq)* for the oppressed, God must "oppress" the mighty, the proud, the oppressors: "Thou hast been a stronghold to the poor, a stronghold to the needy in his distress. . . . Thou dost subdue [*'anah*] the noise of the aliens [or: powerful]; as heat by the shade of a cloud, so the song of the ruthless is stilled" (Isa. 25:4–5).[16]

So, too, when Israel itself becomes an oppressor nation and when privileged classes within the country practice oppression with utter disregard, Yahweh will reject the house of David, destroy the alliance it has contracted, and humiliate (*'anah* in the sense of dishonor, abase) the royal line: he will hand Israel over to spoilers (1 Kings 11:39; 2 Kings 17:20). Such is the vengeance Yahweh exacts on behalf of the oppressed.

The other contexts in which God appears as the active subject of the verb *'anah* are those in which God brings the people into submission so that they will follow the divine laws that seek the good of humankind.[17]

This verb can also mean "affliction" or "distress."[18]

The word *'anah,* along with *nagash* and *daka'* (which I shall examine further on), appears in one of the songs of the Suffering Servant (Isa. 53:4, 7). The Oppressed Servant, as Hanks calls him, suffered oppression not only in body but in his entire being: he was oppressed and dishonored.

There is a text that is difficult to translate, but one that brings out very well the connection between "oppression" and "affliction (dishonor, degradation)" as related meanings of *'anah.* The chapter—Isaiah 58—to which the text belongs deals with the meaning of a real fast. Here are several versions: "If you distribute your bread to the hungry and satisfy the afflicted soul [*'anah, nephesh*] . . ." (Isa. 58:10, in the *Biblia de Jerusalén* and the *Santa Biblia* [Reina and Valera]; cf. RSV: ". . . and satisfy the desire of the afflicted . . ."); "When you share your bread with the hungry and fill the stomach of the needy [*'anah, nephesh*] . . ." *(Nueva Biblia Española);* "If you give the hungry person what you would desire for yourself and if you satisfy the oppressed person [*'anah, nephesh*] . . ." *(La Biblia para Latinoamérica;* cf. JB: ". . . if you give . . . relief to the oppressed . . .").

It is evidently not the same thing to satisfy an afflicted soul and to satisfy the stomach of the needy and the oppressed. The difficulty in translating the passage is due primarily to the word *nephesh* (being; life; interiority; person . . .) and is complicated by the combination of this word with *'anah.*[19]

The three translations may all be legitimate. The first of the three, however, necessarily presupposes that the persons feel an "affliction *('anah)* of soul" (the idea of interiority) because of the oppression/degradation to which they have been subjected. If, then, the person is to be fully liberated, the liberation must include not only the body (through the satisfaction of basic needs) but also the whole interior dimension of being: the satisfaction of living in a way worthy of a human being.

Nonetheless, even though *nephesh-'anah* can be translated either as "humiliated life" or as "oppressed person," it is very probable that the second half of the verse is parallel to and synonymous with the first half, as is frequently the case in Hebrew poetry. If so, then the better translation is "oppressed person" or "stomach of the oppressed," as in the second and third versions.

3. Oppression causes a people to cry out for liberation (lahats)[20]

The word *lahats* means "oppress," "press (or squeeze),"[21] and "harass (or drive back, or corral)."[22] The substantive form means "oppression."

The basic idea of this root is that of "pressing" or "crushing." The action of crushing elicits a reaction: a cry of pain.

The Egyptian rulers were brutally oppressing *(nagash)* the Hebrews and making harsh, exploitative demands to gain results. This oppression *('anah)* reached into the innermost being of the slaves and of the entire people, and this experience of being crushed *(lahats)* caused them to cry out, to raise a clamor (Exod. 3:9).

Since oppression is obviously a situation that is neither acceptable nor tolerable, a moment comes when the weight of it provokes unrestrained tears, cries of pain, and a call for quick liberation.

In the history of this people, the oppression *(lahats)* that causes them to cry out is due to tangible things; there is no question solely of psychological anguish. A clear example that helps us understand what oppression meant to the Hebrew people is to be found in 1 Kings 22:27 (cf. Isa. 30:20). The verse concerns a "political prisoner" who is being fed on bread and water. His name is Micaiah and he has prophesied against King Ahab, who orders him taken to the governor of the city: "Thus says the king, 'Put this fellow in prison and feed him with [literally, subject him to: *lahats*] scant fare of bread and water, until I come in peace.' "

Analysis shows that in almost all the Old Testament contexts of oppression in which *lahats* occurs, the situation is of this kind: a people lies under the yoke of a stronger nation, and its experience of oppression *(lahats)* causes it to cry out *(tsa'aq)* to God.[23]

Thus, when we compare texts, we often find that passages have one and the same structure: (1) an oppressive situation; (2) outcry; (3) the cry is heard; (4) liberation.

In the time of the Judges, for example, the Hebrews fell repeatedly under the power of other peoples: the Amorites, the Amalekites, the Midianites, the Phoenicians, the Philistines, and so on (Judg. 10:12; 4:3, etc.), and cried out to God.

But the story does not stop with the outcry. Someone hears the cry: Yahweh. Then liberation *(natsal, yasha,* or *'alah)*, the counterpart of oppression, immediately enters the picture.[24] Deuteronomy 26:7 recalls what led to the victory of Israel over Egypt: "Then we *cried* to the Lord the God of our fathers, and the Lord heard our voice, and saw our affliction, our toil, and our oppression *[lahats]*."

In other contexts there is a strong expression of hope in an immediate liberation and in the prospect of a new and just social structure. Thus in the period when the Assyrian empire was expanding, the prophet Jeremiah announces:

> Out of them shall come songs of thanksgiving,
> and the voices of those who make merry. . . .
> Their children shall be as they were of old,
> and their congregation shall be established before me;
> and I will punish all who oppress them *[lahats]*.
> Their prince shall be one of themselves,
> their ruler shall come forth from their midst.
> [Jer. 30:19–21]

The prophet Isaiah goes even further. He never foretells oppression between nation and nation but on the contrary sees all human beings as brothers and sisters. In the process of total liberation these steps will follow one after the other: first, the oppressed people (in this case, Israel) will rise up against its foreign rulers (Isa. 19:17); they will come to know Yahweh, they will *cry out* because of oppression *(lahats;* v. 20), and will be heard and set free. Then, says the prophet,

> In that day there will be a highway from Egypt to Assyria, and the Assyrian will come into Egypt, and the Egyptian into Assyria, and the Egyptians will worship with the Assyrians. In that day Israel will be the third with Egypt and Assyria, a blessing in the midst of the earth, whom the Lord of hosts has blessed, saying, "Blessed be Egypt my people, and Assyria the work of my hands, and Israel my heritage" [Isa. 19:23–24].

In the majority of instances the reason God takes the side of Israel is primarily because it is living under the rule of another and more powerful nation, in wretched conditions as compared with those of its conqueror. Correspondingly, when we see oppression gaining the upper hand in Israel, when this nation itself becomes an oppressor, God abandons the oppressor class and rescues the lowly and the poor.[25] " 'I will raise up against you a nation, O house of Israel,' says the Lord, the God of hosts; 'and they shall oppress you [*lahats*] . . .' " (Amos 6:14).

The oppressors do not deserve forgiveness and in fact cannot be forgiven without first paying for their sin: "If I ever. . . repaid a friend evil for good, spared [*halats*] a man who wronged me [*tsarar*] . . ." (Ps. 7:4, JB). The Hebrew text here contains a serious mistake due to a transposition of letters: the reading should be *halats* (forgive, spare) and not *lahats* (oppress, plunder).[26]

NOTES

1. The roots I omit are: *dahaq, shod, homets, avatah, tsarar* and its homonym, and *'otser.* In one or another manner the lexicons define them as oppression. I should, however, mention three of the seven roots which I do not

analyze, since these three are quite prominent in some texts: (1) *tsarar,* "to be an enemy," "to be an adversary," "to be hostile to"; (2) a homonym of the first, another *tsarar,* which literally means "to tie" or "to bind" and in its intransitive use "to be narrow," "to be in need" (F. H. W. Gesenius, *A Hebrew and English Lexicon of the Old Testament,* ed. Francis Brown, S. R. Driver, and Charles A. Briggs [Oxford: Clarendon Press, 1952], p. 783); and (3) *'otser* (a masculine noun), meaning "coercion," "oppression" (Koehler-Baumgartner, *Lexicon in Veteris Testamenti Libros* 2nd ed. [Leiden: E.J. Brill, 1958], p. 729). While these words do have a more general meaning, the strong connotation of oppression that they carry in some contexts is quite clear. Versions of the Bible at times translate these three terms as "oppress/oppression." Some texts in which the three occur: (1) *tsarar I:* Amos 5:12; Ps. 69:20; 7:5; 143:12; (2) *tsarar II:* Isa. 25:4; Ps. 31:10; (3) *'otser:* Ps. 107:39; Isa. 53:8.

2. The word occurs about twenty times in the Old Testament, mostly in Isaiah.

3. Tomás Hanks, "La opresion y la pobreza en la teología bíblica," *Estudios Ecuménicos* 32/78 (Mexico City, CEE):23.

4. Ibid.

5. The text deals with the remission, required by law every seventh year, of every citizen's debts.

6. When v. 3 goes on to say that "you may exact payment [bring pressure on/oppress] a foreigner," the reference is not to an immigrant *(ger)* but to a visiting foreigner.

7. See the note in the *Biblia de Jerusalén.*

8. *Reina and Valera:* "And the people will do violence to one another." *Biblia de Jerusalén:* "The people will bully each other, neighbor and neighbor"; cf. JB, Eng. version. *Nueva Biblia española:* "The people will attack one another." *Biblia latinoamericana:* "The people will molest one another." In English see also, for example, RSV: "And the people will oppress one another"; NEB: "The people shall deal harshly each man with his fellow and with his neighbor." Note the same difficulty with the *Niphal* in 1 Samuel 13:6.

9. The word occurs about eighty times, mostly in the Psalms.

10. For the idea of *oppress:* Gen. 15:13; 17:6; 31:50; Exod. 1:11, 12; 22:21ff.; Num. 24:24; Deut. 26:6; 1 Sam. 12:8; 2 Sam. 7:10; Ps. 89:23; 94:5; 105:18; Job 30:11; 37:23; Isa. 58:10; 60:14; Ezek. 22:29; Zeph. 3:19. *Humiliate, degrade, lower:* 1 Kings 8:35; 11:39; 2 Chron. 6:26; Ps. 55:20; 116:10; Isa. 25:5; Dan. 10:12; Zech. 10:1; Isa. 53:4,7. *Dominate, subdue:* Gen. 16:9; Exod. 10:3; Judg. 16:5; Ezra 8:21; Ps. 119:67, 107; Isa. 31:4. *Afflict, distress:* Deut. 8:2; 1 Kings 2:26; Ps. 35:13; 90:15. *Violate, force* (a woman): Gen. 34:2; Deut. 21:14; 22:24; 22:29; Judg. 19:24; 20:5; 2 Sam. 13:12; Ezek. 22:10, 11. *Fast:* Lev. 23:29; Num. 29:7; Isa. 58:3, 5.

11. The (Spanish) versions of the Bible often translate the word as "humili- ate." Hanks observes: "More than any other word, *'anah* expresses something of the profound psychological experience resulting from oppression" (Hanks, "La opresión," p. 29).

12. Koehler-Baumgartner, *Lexicon,* p. 719.

13. See, for example, Deut. 8:2; 1 Kings 8:35; 11:39; 2 Kings 17:20; 2 Chron. 6:26; Isa. 25:5; Ps. 55:22; 119:75, 71.

14. See the references in n. 10, above, for "violate, force."

15. See Ezra 12:8; Dan. 10:12; Ps. 119:67. Note also how the people accept God's command to humble themselves and follow his teaching. There is an apparent exception in Gen. 16:9, where Hagar, a slave woman, is to submit to

her mistress, despite everything; but there is a difference, since a plan exists which includes this submission and turns it to the good of the majority. Hagar is to submit to this plan and so be blessed.

16. God oppresses: see, for example, Zeph. 3:19; Ps. 89:23, 24. Other verses use different terms: 1 Kings 11:39; Isa. 25:5; Ps. 55:22. This verb and *daka'* are possibly the only ones that can have God as the active subject.

17. Deut. 8:2; Ps. 119:71, 75; 1 Kings 8:35; 2 Chron. 6:26.

18. Ps. 90:15; Deut. 8:2; 1 Kings 2:26; Ps. 35:13; 116:10.

19. Note the intense love required if fasting is to be genuine. It is not just any food that is distributed but the food by which the givers sustain themselves *(naphshka)*. *Nephesh* can also mean "desire" or "appetite." This is the meaning which the *Biblia para Latinoamérica* gives to the first *nephesh* in the verse.

20. The word occurs some twenty-four times, especially in Psalms, Judges, and Exodus.

21. In the Old Testament "press" in the literal sense occurs very rarely. In Num. 22:25 Balaam's ass presses *(lahats)* his rider's foot against the wall. In 2 Kings 6:32 Elisha orders the elders to *shut* the door against the messengers of the king.

22. The idea of "driving" or "putting pressure on" is to be seen in Judg. 1:34 where the Amorites drive *(lahats)* the Danites back into the hills.

23. See Judg. 2:18; 4:3; 2 Kings 13:4; Isa. 19:20.

24. See Judg. 2:18; 4:3; 6:7; 10:12; 2 Kings 13:4; 1 Sam. 10:18, 19; Ps. 56:2; Jer. 30:20; Isa. 19:20.

25. Jer. 52:15; Zeph. 2:3.

26. Corrected by Ubach and Gunkel; see Ricardo Arconada, "Salmos," in *La Sagrada Escritura: Antiguo Testamento* (Madrid: BAC, 1969), 4:38. Also corrected by Manuel Revuelta in *Biblia de Jerusalén* (cf., in English, JB and NEB). The verse alludes to the law of talion, the original intention of which was, on the one hand, to protect the members of the inferior social class and, on the other, "to provide equality before the law from acts of physical violence. The wealthy could no longer escape punishment for their crime by simply paying a fine." Later Jewish midrash reinterpreted the law to mean that monetary recompense could indeed be made for a life or an eye. See Brevard S. Childs, *The Book of Exodus* (Philadelphia: Westminster, 1975), p. 472.

Chapter 2

Oppression at the National Level

The biblical narratives tell us that after the Hebrews had been freed from the yoke of Egyptian rule, they gradually established themselves as an ever more powerful nation and finally chose monarchical rule. Israel then became itself an oppressor (Samuel had predicted this; see 1 Sam. 8:11–18). On the one hand, it expanded its domain at the cost of poorer and weaker peoples and exacted tribute from them. On the other, the rulers and influential groups within Israel became major oppressors of their own country and impoverished the lowly of the nation.

In Chapter 1 I analyzed three words for oppression as these occurred in contexts in which one nation oppressed another entire people. Now I will examine the remaining Hebrew roots, but in contexts in which the oppression is exercised by a privileged, ruling group within a nation. I do not mean to imply that the earlier three terms occur only in contexts of oppression of one people by another, nor that the remaining six may not be used in contexts of oppression at the international level. The various terms are sometimes used interchangeably in passages marked by parallelism; at times, too, they are used synonymously. The division I am adopting is meant simply to bring out the fact that there are two different types of oppression to be seen in the history of nations. In addition, I think that when the linguistic data are organized in this manner, a certain consistency in the use of terms emerges, as can be seen from the story of the Exodus.

Psalm 72 enables us to situate three of the words used for

oppression: *'ashaq, daka',* and *tok*. The psalm is speaking of oppression within the nation.

> Give the king thy justice, O God,
>   and thy righteousness to the royal son!
> May he judge thy people with righteousness,
>   and thy poor with justice!
> Let the mountains bear prosperity for the people,
>   and the hills, in righteousness!
> May he defend the cause of the poor of the people,
>   give deliverance to the needy,
>   and crush [*daka'*] the oppressor [*'ashaq*]!
> May he live while the sun endures,
>   and as long as the moon,
>   throughout all generations!
> May he be like rain that falls on the mown grass,
>   like showers that water the earth!
> In his days may righteousness flourish,
>   and peace abound, till the moon be no more! . . .
> For he delivers the needy when he calls,
>   the poor and him who has no helper.
> He has pity on the weak and the needy,
>   and saves the lives of the needy.
> From oppression [*tok*] and violence he redeems their life;
>   and precious is their blood in his sight. . . .
> May there be abundance of grain in the land;
>   on the tops of the mountains may it wave;
>   may its fruit be like Lebanon;
> and may men blossom forth from the cities
>   like the grass of the field!
> May his name endure for ever,
>   his fame continue as long as the sun!
> May men bless themselves by him,
>   all nations call him blessed!

This beautiful Hebrew poem is a prayer uttered by the poor among the people who are oppressed by a rich, powerful, and influential class.[1] They are asking for judgment (*mishpat*) and justice (*tsedeq*).

Another psalm containing similar sentiments makes use of

still another word for oppression: *dak*. "Let not the downtrodden [*dak*] be put to shame; let the poor and needy praise thy name" (Ps. 74:21).

Many times throughout the history of Israel, whether in the period of the united kingdom (Judah and Israel) or in the period of division, these structures of injustice make their appearance. In other words, within this nation, especially once it was no longer under the direct control of any foreign power, the poor were cruelly oppressed and exploited by their own people.

Here is the situation in the time of the prophet Ezekiel: "The people of the land [or: landowners] have practiced extortion [*'ashaq*] and committed robbery [*gazal*]; they have oppressed [*yanah*] the poor and needy, and have extorted [*'ashaq*] from the sojourner without redress" (Ezek. 22:29).[2] Here another of our nine words for oppression makes its appearance: *yanah*.

Amos addresses himself as follows to the women of the oppressor class: "Hear this word, you cows of Bashan, who are in the mountains of Samaria, who oppress [*'ashaq*] the poor, who crush [*ratsats*] the needy" (Amos 4:1).[3] Here, in parallelism with *'ashaq*, is the ninth word for oppression: *ratsats*.

I shall examine these words in turn, with a view to determining the special nuances of each.

1. The rich oppress the poor in order to rob them (*'ashaq*)[4]

This word is used often in the Old Testament; indeed, it can even be said that "the most important and basic Hebrew words that express the experience of oppression come from the verb *'ashaq*."[5]

The verb means "oppress," "obtain by violence," "extort." "The verb signifies various forms of injustice and violence by which the rich oppress the poor: economic exploitation, unjust sentences, arbitrary administrative actions, and violent means."[6]

Thus at least four basic ideas cluster around this root: injustice, violence, robbery or theft, and poverty.

When injustice manifests itself in every aspect of a nation's life, we necessarily infer that the structures of violence are being condoned by the authorities or by influential persons such as rulers, prophets, priests, and the wealthy. This verse from Ecclesiastes is one of many passages that link oppression and injustice, as well as poverty and violence: "If in a province you see the *poor* oppressed [*'ashaq*], *right* and *justice violated*, do not be surprised. You will be told that officials are under the supervision of superiors, who are supervised in turn; you will hear talk of the service of the king" (Eccles. 5:8, JB).

Since one meaning of the verb *'ashaq* is "to extort," it is easy to see that it has strong overtones of "despoliation." *'ashaq* is in fact often accompanied by the word *gazal*, which means "to despoil, rob."[7] "As for his father because he practiced extortion [*'ashaq*], robbed [*gazal*] his brother. . ." (Ezek. 18:18).

The prophet Micah denounces the unjust actions of the oppressor class in Judah (Mic. 2:1–2).[8]

The oppressor *robs* the oppressed in different ways: by using false scales (fraud) (Hos. 12:7); by holding back the laborer's wages (Jer. 22:13); by bribery, usury, and profit at a neighbor's expense (Ezek. 22:7, 12).

Such perversions of justice by oppressors have a direct effect on the lives of the oppressed. In fact, the actions are deadly in their effect once they seize the poor person's means of subsistence. The following saying from the Book of Proverbs shows the relationship between the four elements of *'ashaq*: "A wicked man who *oppresses* [*'ashaq*] the *poor:* here is a *devastating* [violence] rain—and *farewell, bread* [robbery]" (28:3, JB).

The Mosaic code uses *'ashaq* with some frequency;[9] the articles prohibiting oppression connect *'ashaq* with exploitation and thus clearly refer to robbery or despoliation. For example: "You shall not oppress [*'ashaq*] your neighbor or rob [*gazal*] him. The wages of a hired servant shall not remain with you all night until the morning" (Lev. 19:13).

We may say, then, that "oppressed" is synonymous with "despoiled," and "despoiled" with "poor." Some versions even translate the substantive of *gazal* at times by "oppressed": "Thus says Yahweh: Practice right and justice, liberate the oppressed [*gazal*] from the hands of the oppressor [*'ashaq*]" (Jer. 22:3 in the *Biblia de Jerusalén*; cf. 21:12).

There is, then, a fairly obvious correlation between the oppressor and the poor. And when the question of how the act of oppression impoverishes the oppressed is asked, the answer that emerges from an analysis of *'ashaq* (and of other words, too, as we shall see further on) is that oppression involves violent robbery, despoliation.

The reason for this is that oppressors do not oppress because they are cruel or enjoy it. They do not act violently because they have an aggressive temperament; they do not rob for the sake of robbing. Their primary purpose is to accumulate wealth, and it is possible to accumulate wealth only by robbing one's neighbor and committing acts of violence and injustice.

In these texts of oppression the proverbs and poems of the humble folk show that they know God as liberator and defender of their cause. They say, for example: the Lord is he "who executes justice [*tsedeq*] for the oppressed [*'ashaq*]; who gives food to the hungry" (Ps. 146:7; cf. 72:4; and note the connection between justice and oppression and between robbery and gift).

In some texts oppression of the poor is equated with an act of oppression against God (see Lev. 5:21 [6:1]; Prov. 14:31).

2. Oppression dehumanizes the poor *(daka')*[10]

Psalm 72, which I cited at length above, speaks of a just ruler who will rescue the children of the poor and crush (*daka'*) the oppressor (*'osheq*). *Daka'* is frequently found in its piel (intensive) form, meaning "to grind, pulverize, crush" (Ps. 89:11). In its other stems (except the qal) the verb appears in the passive voice: "to be oppressed, crushed, worn out, knocked down, grieved." In its substantival or adjectival form the root means "bruised, crushed" (Isa. 53:10), or "contrite" (Isa. 57:15);[11] in the second of these two texts the term is parallel with, and reinforces, the word *shaphal,* "humbled." In Psalm 90:3 it can be translated as "dust."[12]

In Deuteronomy 23:1 [23:2] the word has a somewhat different meaning, but one that helps us realize how severe a form injustice can take. Baumgartner in fact regards the word here as a homonym and suggests "castrated" (German: *entmannt*) as a translation; the man is castrated by having his testicles crushed.[13]

Daka' seems to be the strongest of the Hebrew words for oppression.[14] It is worth noting that on various occasions *daka'* appears in the company of *nagash* and *'anah* (see Isa. 53; Ps. 94:4), which I analyzed in Chapter 1 and which mean, respectively, "to oppress with violence" and "to oppress to the point of degrading the person." I believe that *daka'* includes both these notions in their strongest sense.

When the poet cries out to Yahweh in Psalm 94:5 and says, "They crush [*daka'*] thy people, O Lord, and afflict ['*anah*] thy heritage," we know that the people are suffering from the deepest and most inhuman effects of oppression.

The direct object or complement of the action received from the verb *daka'* is in most instances the person as a whole, whether it be an individual or the people of Yahweh; but there are passages in which the direct object is the heart (*leb*) or the soul, or spirit (*ruah*) (Isa. 57:15). In these latter cases there is question of discouragement, consternation (or dismay), or of being crushed (see Jer. 44:10; Isa. 19:10).

But in the texts I have examined I note that this discouragement of heart does not appear in isolation. Generally it is caused by prior acts of oppression and injustice. For example, the prophet Isaiah in Chapters 56 and 57 is launching a sharp attack on the unworthy rulers of Judah.[15] These men, he says, are "dogs [that] have a mighty appetite" (56:11); in these unjust times the righteous perish, and no one minds (57:1). But, Isaiah points out, all this will come to an end, because Yahweh says: "I dwell in the high and holy place, and also with him who is of a contrite [*daka'*] and humble [*shaphal*] spirit [*ruah*], to revive the spirit of the humble, and to revive the heart of the contrite [*daka'*]" (Isa. 57:15).

It follows that when oppression is ruthless (*daka'*) it reaches into the innermost being of the person. The oppressed suffer oppression in their bodies and in their interior selves. The result is a high degree of dehumanization and depersonalization. It is necessary to revive "the spirit of the humble," and this requires recalling concrete promises, as in Isaiah 57:13: "He who takes refuge in me shall possess the land, and shall inherit my holy mountain."[16]

It is worth noting that this verb has a place in the liberating action of Yahweh, who "crushes the oppressor": "Knowing their works, he overturns them [the mighty] in the night, and they are crushed" (Job 34:25); he bruises the Suffering Servant (Isa. 53:10).[17] The words '*anah* and *daka'* are almost the only verbs of this type in which God appears as the active subject.

The oppressors (*'osheq*) will themselves suffer crushing oppression (*daka'*) if they continue to act cruelly and unjustly (Ps. 72:4).

3. Oppression is surrounded by lies *(tok)*

In Psalm 72:14, as I noted earlier, the Hebrew word *tok* is used for "oppression": "From oppression [*tok*]and violence he redeems their life; and precious is their blood in his sight." Here it is the poor who will obtain liberation and a better life when a just ruler comes (cf. Ps. 72:13).

This word is very rare in the Old Testament (it is used four times) and means "oppression, tyranny." It is a masculine noun derived from the verb *takak* (not used in the Old Testament). In Proverbs 29:13 *tok* appears in the plural with *'ish* ("person") and is translated as "oppressor" or "tyrant."

In addition to showing a direct relationship between oppression and poverty, in two of its four uses this word points to a situation of oppression/deception. These two passages from the Psalms speak of falsehood, deception, lying. Oppression [*tok*] and fraud do not depart from its [the city's] market place (Ps. 55:11); "His mouth is filled with cursing and deceit and oppression; under his tongue are mischief and iniquity [*tok*]" (Ps. 10:7).

4. Oppression exists but there is also hope *(dak)*

Dak is derived from the verb *dakak*,[18] which means "to wear out" by rubbing.[19] The verb is rare and unusual. *Dak* (a masculine adjective) means, basically, "oppressed" or "wretched." It is usually translated as "oppressed," "troubled," or "downtrodden." *Dak* is closely related in meaning to *daka'*, since wearing something away by rubbing it is a form of pulverization.

The word appears approximately six times, chiefly in the Psalms.[20] The situation in each of the texts is similar: the poor lift their voices to God in a prayer for speedy justice. "Let not the downtrodden [*dak*] be put to shame; let the poor and needy praise thy name" (Ps. 74:21). "O Lord, thou wilt hear the desire of the meek; thou wilt strengthen their heart, thou wilt incline thy ear to do justice to the fatherless and the oppressed [*dak*], so

that man who is of earth may strike terror no more" (Ps.
10:17–18). "The Lord is a stronghold for the oppressed [*dak*], a
stronghold in times of trouble" (Ps. 9:9). "Arise, O Lord; O
God, lift up thy hand; forget not the afflicted [or: oppressed,
dak]" (Ps. 10:12).

In these four contexts there is a definite note of hope in the
establishment of a new order of things. When the element of
hope is present, even though oppression may be at its most intense, there is the expectation of the emergence of a new humanity. Yahweh is revealed as the hope which makes possible the
struggle for a new order of things.[21]

5. The oppressor enslaves and kills the oppressed (yanah)[22]

The prophets Ezekiel and Zephaniah violently attack the oppressor class for its acts of injustice.[23] Speaking of Jerusalem,
Zephaniah says: "Woe to her that is rebellious and defiled, the
oppressing [*yanah*] city!" (3:1).

The root *yanah* means "to oppress, exploit, dominate in a
brutal way; to suppress; put an end to, despoil; to deceive,
cheat" (see Lev. 25:14).[24] Von Rad suggests as the literal meaning
"to enslave."[25]

The term can be used as a parallel to *'ashaq* (see Jer. 22:3;
Ezek. 22:7; 22:29) and to *lahats* (Exod. 22:20).

The word has strong overtones of robbery, despoliation, and
deadly violence.

The situations in which Ezekiel and Zephaniah use the term
are situations of death. Jerusalem is said to be defiled by blood
(Zeph. 3:1; Ezek. 22:3) because of the many innocent people
whose deaths are the result of oppression. The oppression itself
is the result of collusion among rulers, judges, prophets, and
priests.

The chief motive for this oppression that goes as far as murder
is more than simply evil; it is killing in order to rob and thus
obtain greater wealth. *Gazal* is frequently used as the aim of this
oppression.

This oppression by rulers and subordinate leaders is deadly;
each of these authorities, according to his power (Hebrew: his
arm), is bent on spilling innocent blood (Ezek. 22:6). The rulers

have accepted bribes; they "have taken treasure and precious things, . . . destroying lives to get dishonest gain" (Ezek. 22:25, 28).The landowners "have practiced extortion and committed robbery; they have oppressed [*yanah*] the poor" (22:29). In short, the entire ruling class conspires against the powerless, oppressing (*yanah*) them to the point of killing them in order to acquire what they have.

Ezekiel defines the righteous person as one who "does not oppress [*yanah*] any one, but restores to the debtor his pledge, commits no robbery [*gazal*], gives his bread to the hungry and covers the naked with a garment" (Ezek. 18:7). And in the anticipated new society he foresees a redistribution of the land which the powerful have stolen: "The prince shall not take any of the inheritance of the people, thrusting [*yanah*] them out of their property" (Ezek. 46:18); "And my princes shall no more oppress [*yanah*] my people; but they shall let the house of Israel have the land according to their tribes" (Ezek. 45:8).

In the laws of the Torah the term *yanah* is sometimes used in the sense of "enslave,"[26] and at other times with the connotation of robbery.[27] An example of *yanah* as "enslave": "You shall not wrong [i.e., enslave: *yanah*] a stranger [*ger*] or oppress [*lahats*] him, for you were strangers in the land of Egypt" (Exod. 22:21). In this passage Luther translates *yanah* as *schinden*, which means "to force with hard labor." An example of *yanah* with the connotation of robbery: "If you sell to your neighbor or buy from your neighbor, you shall not wrong one another [wrong = *yanah*, in the sense of "cheat"]" (Lev. 25:14).

6. The poor are ground down so that they may be robbed (*ratsats*)[28]

In the time of Jehoiakim, king of Judah, there was a great deal of injustice found in Israelite society. The prophet Jeremiah accuses Jehoiakim: "You have eyes and heart only for your dishonest gain [*gasa'*], for shedding innocent blood, and for practicing oppression ['*ashaq*] and violence [*ratsats*]" (22:17).[29] The verb *ratsats* means, literally, "mash, grind, crush." Thus we read of the "broken reed" (Isa. 36:6; 2 Kings 18:21) and the "crushed skull" (Judg. 9:53; Ps. 74:14).

The word is nonetheless used frequently in the Old Testament in the sense of "oppression." Under this heading the lexicons translate it as "oppress forcibly, crush." In its intensive (piel) form it means "oppress grievously."[30]

In various texts the word appears as parallel to *'ashaq* or *lahats.*[31]

An analysis of the texts and the Hebrew words used shows that these terms can be found in the context of oppression between nations or in that of oppression within a nation. Thus, *'ashaq*, for example, appears mainly in the context of injustices within a country, as does *yanah. Lahats* and *nagash*, on the other hand, tend generally, but not always, to refer to oppression on the international level. *Ratsats* is used with the same frequency in connection with both levels of oppression.[32]

The word *gazal*, "robbery, despoliation," can be linked with *ratsats* as it can with other words for "oppression" that we have seen. "For he has crushed [*ratsats*] and abandoned the poor, he has seized [*gazal*] a house which he did not build" (Job 20:19). The "he" in this text is the wicked man (*rash*) who piles up wealth (Job 20:15, 20).

In his fifty-eighth chapter, the prophet Isaiah draws a contrast between the kind of fasting that focuses primarily on the humbling of the self before God (*'anah*, *nephesh*) and a more authentic fasting which calls for complete obedience and the full surrender of the person: "Is not this the fast that I choose: to loose the bonds of wickedness, to undo the thongs of the yoke, to let the oppressed [*ratsats*] go free, and to break every yoke?" (Isa. 58:6).

Righteousness requires, therefore, that we undo yokes and free those who are bound by them, the *ratsutsim*. But the fasting does not end there. It calls for a still more profound struggle in which we seek to *tear out at the roots the reasons for all the yokes* that exist in society and get rid of them.

NOTES

1. The psalm is pre-exilic and was composed for the coronation of an Israelite king. It is probably to be regarded as one of the "royal psalms"; see Mitchell Dahood, *Psalms II*, Anchor Bible 17 (Garden City, N.Y.: Doubleday, 1968), p. 179.

2. Ezekiel (ministry: ca. 593–571) experienced the Babylonian exile.

3. Amos preached in Samaria and at Bethel, ca. 760 B.C., when Jeroboam II was king of Israel. The priest Amaziah had him banished for his stern denunciations of the king and the rich people of the land.

4. The word occurs some sixty times, mostly in the Psalms and in the prophets Isaiah, Jeremiah, and Ezekiel.

5. See Tomás Hanks, "La opresión y la pobreza en la teología bíblica," *Estudios Ecuménicos* 32/78 (Mexico City, CEE): 18.

6. F. Buck, "Malaquías," in *La Sagrada Escritura: Antiguo Testamento* (Madrid: BAC, 1971), 6:591.

7. *'ashaq* with *gazal*: see, for example, Lev. 5:21; Eccles. 5:7; Ezek. 22:29; 18:18; Mic. 2:1–2.

8. Micah was from a poor peasant family; he preached against social injustice in Samaria and Jerusalem (740–686 B.C.).

9. See, for example, Lev. 5:21; 19:13; Deut. 24:14; Jer. 22:3; 7:6; Zech. 7:10.

10. The word occurs some twenty-five times, notably in Isaiah, Psalms, and Job.

11. Walter Baumgartner, *Hebräisches und Aramäisches Lexikon zum Alten Testament*, 3rd ed. (Leiden: Brill, 1974), 1:212.

12. Ibid.

13. Ibid.

14. See also, Hanks, "La opresión," p. 28.

15. Isaiah (ca. 741–701 B.C.) prophesied during the crisis caused by the expansion of the Assyrian empire.

16. Another example: Isa. 19:10. Other types of oppressed persons: Ps. 34:19; 143:3.

17. See also, for example, Ps. 90:3; Isa. 19:10.

18. And not from *daka'*, as Hanks thinks; see F. H. W. Gesenius, *Hebrew and English Lexicon of the Old Testament*, ed. Francis Brown, S. R. Driver, and Charles A. Briggs (Oxford: Clarendon Press, 1952), p. 194.

19. In German, *zerreiben*; see Baumgartner, *Hebräisches und Aramäisches Lexikon*, 1:212.

20. Ps. 9:9; 10:18; 74:21; Sir. 42. Doubtful in Prov. 26:28 and Ps. 10:12.

21. See Chapter 5, below.

22. *Yanah* occurs about twenty times, mostly in Ezekiel.

23. Zephaniah attacked injustice in Judah ca. 630 B.C. He was a contemporary of the prophet Jeremiah.

24. Baumgartner, *Hebräisches und Aramäisches Lexikon*, 2:398.

25. Gerhard von Rad, *Deuteronomy: A Commentary* (Philadelphia: Westminster, 1966), p. 147; also cited by Hanks, "La opresión," p. 21.

26. Exod. 22:20; Lev. 19:33; Deut. 23:17.

27. Lev. 25:14, 17.

28. The word occurs some nineteen times, mostly in Isaiah.

29. Jeremiah (626–587 B.C.) attacked injustice at Jerusalem; for criticizing the king, the prophets, and the priests he suffered threats, persecution, and imprisonment.

30. See Gesenius, *Hebrew and English Lexicon*, p. 954.

31. With *'ashaq*: Deut. 28:33; 1 Sam. 12:3; Amos 4:1; with *lahats*: Judg. 10:8, 12.

32. Oppression within a nation: see, for example, Job 20:19; Amos 4:1; oppression between nations: see, for example, Judg. 10:12; Isa. 29:7.

Chapter 3

The Agents and the Objects of Oppression: Oppressors and Oppressed

Whenever there is talk of oppression in the Bible, or anywhere, it is important to identify and locate those involved in it as oppressors and as oppressed. Otherwise there is danger of regarding oppression as simply one more theme in the discussion of justice and freedom, and no substantial analysis will be made of the motives, activities, and persons of those who cause this evil state of injustice. As long as the characteristic traits of oppressors have not been identified and assigned, even the oppressor will be able to speak out against oppression. The oppressed, for their part, may regard oppression as an unjust and deplorable state but one that is the result of some natural historical determinism. Then both oppressors and oppressed will be responsible for the oppression.[1]

Another indispensable part of my investigation is the discovery of the various methods or forms of oppression. The behavior of the oppressor is a great help in describing the subject (or agent) and object (the "recipients") of oppression, getting at the real meaning of oppression, and making concrete Christian choices in the face of this reality.

In this chapter, then, I shall try to describe those actively and passively involved in oppression, and then, in Chapter 4, to identify the methods and forms of oppression.

The Oppressors

General Characteristics

As we saw in the previous chapter, the Old Testament acknowledges two levels or areas of oppression: an international level, where a powerful nation oppresses a weaker nation; and a national level, where unjust structures mark life within a single nation.

On both levels, however, certain characteristic traits are common to all oppressors in almost all situations.

1. They are rich and strive to increase their wealth.

In most cases the desire for greater wealth is the chief reason for oppression. Oppressors do not care how they obtain what they desire; there is no room for morality in their hearts. They covet whatever they see, and spend their time thinking up unjust ways of increasing their wealth (Mic. 2:1-2).

Tyre was a proud commercial city that controlled the sea and had great revenues pouring in from distant lands (Isa. 23:3, 7). The prophet Isaiah tells the city that chastisement is imminent: Yahweh will destroy its source of wealth, its proud harbor. But, because of Yahweh's love, Tyre will rise again and engage anew in trade with all the nations. However, there will be a major difference: "Her merchandise and her hire will be dedicated to the Lord; *it will not be stored or hoarded*, but her merchandise will supply abundant food and fine clothing for those who dwell before the Lord" (Isa. 23:18).[2]

The corrupt leaders of Samaria follow in the footsteps of the pagan nations. Therefore Yahweh cannot walk at their side: "Do two walk together unless they have made an appointment?" (Amos 3:3). Samaria is full of disorder and violence: " 'They do not know how to do right,' says the Lord, 'those who store up violence and robbery in their strongholds' " (Amos 3:10).

The accumulation of wealth for its own sake is unjust, since it amounts to a despoliation of others; the wealth is "stolen treasure."

The texts show us that God is against any hoarding. Jeremiah's oracle against Babylon is very clear: "O you who dwell by many waters, rich in treasures, your end has come, the thread of your life is cut" (Jer. 51:13). And Isaiah: "Behold, I am stirring up the Medes against them [the Babylonians], who have no regard for silver and do not delight in gold" (Isa. 13:17).

We must be clear on one point: it is not the accumulation of wealth as such that draws the condemnation, but rather the fact that every such accumulation entails the despoliation and impoverishment of others.

The belly of the oppressor, says Zophar the Naamathite, is never full; his desires embrace everything (Job 20). "He has crushed [*ratsats*] and abandoned the poor, he has seized [*gazal*] a house which he did not build" (v. 19).

2. Oppressors have power and mastery because they belong to the governing class or are allied with it.

"Woe to those who devise wickedness and work evil upon their beds! When the morning dawns, they perform it, *because it is in the power of their hand*" (Mic. 2:1).

We are faced here with an "institutionalized violence" that receives legitimacy from the established order in which the ruling class is a principal participant: "Hear, you heads of the house of Jacob and rulers of the house of Israel! Is it not for you to know justice?—you . . . who tear the skin off my people . . . and break their bones in pieces, and chop them up like meat in a kettle, like flesh in a caldron" (Mic. 3:1-3).[3]

Under this kind of oppressive regime many of the prophets betray their mission, justifying what is unjust or remaining silent about it or preaching whatever suits them: "Thus says the Lord concerning the prophets who *lead my people astray*, who cry 'Peace' when they have something to eat, but declare war against him who puts nothing in their mouths" (Mic. 3:5). "In the prophets of Jerusalem I have seen a horrible thing: they commit adultery and walk in lies; they strengthen the hands of evildoers" (Jer. 23:14).

3. Oppressors are idolaters.

Generally speaking, in all the biblical texts that speak of oppression, either idols or contempt for Yahweh also make an appearance. All the pagan nations that oppress Israel have their own gods.[4] Against these the prophets level sharp criticism, for these are gods made by human beings, and they are false (Jer.

51:17); they "cannot profit or save, for they are vain" (1 Sam. 12:21). In addition, these false gods do not attack oppression, as Yahweh does; on the contrary, they give it a certain legitimacy, since they do not see it or hear it and cannot speak. Human beings must beg and grovel before them: "They bow down to the work of their hands, . . . so man is humbled, and men are brought low" (Isa. 2:8, 9).

The oppressors never regard Yahweh as God, because they need other gods who will lend justification to their sinful deeds. Yahweh demands that justice be done and hates oppression; therefore the oppressors will not serve Yahweh as God: "Woe to those who hide deep from the Lord their counsel, whose deeds are in the dark, and who say, 'Who sees us? Who knows us?' You turn things upside down!" (Isa. 29:15).

The oppressors and Yahweh do not see eye to eye. For this reason the wicked must deny Yahweh, if only implicitly through their actions: "The wicked boasts of the desires of his heart, and the man greedy for gain curses and renounces the Lord. In the pride of his countenance the wicked does not seek him; all his thoughts are, 'There is no God' " (Ps. 10:3-4).

When the Israelites began to imitate the pagan nations, abandoning Yahweh and taking other gods for themselves, then the state began to turn oppressive. Note the connection between oppression and idolatry in this passage:

> Thus says the Lord God: A city that sheds blood in the
> midst of her, that her time may come, and that makes idols
> to defile herself! . . . Behold, the princes of Israel in you,
> every one according to his power, have been bent on shed-
> ding blood. . . . The sojourner suffers extortion ['ashaq]
> in your midst; the fatherless and the widow are wronged
> ['anah] in you [Ezek. 22:3, 6-7].

There is also a significant connection between idolatry and the accumulation of wealth. Yahweh rejects Israel because "they strike hands with foreigners. Their land is filled with silver and gold, and there is no end to their treasures. . . . Their land is filled with idols; they bow down to the work of their hands" (Isa. 2:6-8). This is why Yahweh is against "all the ships of Tarshish and all things of price. . . . Human pride will be humbled. . . . Yahweh alone will be exalted on that day, and all idols thrown down" (Isa. 2:16–18, JB).

With regard to the fall of Babylon Jeremiah says: "A sword upon all her treasures, that they may be plundered! . . . For it is a land of images, and they are mad over idols" (Jer. 50:37–38).

Those who strive to accumulate riches cannot follow Yahweh. The New Testament sees God and money (mammon) as mutually exclusive divinities; Jesus says that it is impossible to serve two contrary masters at the same time, namely, God and money (Matt. 6:24).

Raúl Vidales is correct, therefore, when he writes that the basic accusation of the prophets against the privileged classes is that they are "idolaters" and "apostates." Vidales connects oppression with idolatry: "They abandoned the original plan and its utopian goal of freedom and began instead to build Israel after the slavery-based model of the neighboring powers. Their religion became a religion of 'fetishes,' a religion of false gods that enslave and kill: the fetishes of anti-utopia and subjection."[5]

In keeping with Matthew 6:24, Vidales also connects idolatry and the accumulation of wealth: "Jesus . . . personifies money as a 'false god.' He is in fact condemning a concrete phenomenon: the accumulation of wealth by injustice and violence."[6]

Let me now identify the oppressors by name.

The International Level

As everyone knows, the Israelite nation experienced oppression at various periods of its history, and sometimes for many years at a time. The Bible tells us of the painful situation of Israel and Judah under the rule of the Egyptians, Assyrians, Babylonians, Persians, Greeks, and Romans. It also tells us of frequent oppression by neighboring peoples during the period of the Judges (the Philistines, Amalekites, Midianites, Phoenicians, and others).[7] The experience of oppression in Egypt is the one that had the greatest formative influence on the tradition of the Hebrew people. This was not only because the cruelty of the oppression was so vivid a memory to the Israelites, but perhaps even more because it exemplified the whole struggle that leads to complete liberation.

But the Israelite nation did not only *suffer* oppression. When it became a great nation, it too turned oppressor; it expanded its empire and dominated other, weaker peoples—conquering, enslaving, imposing tribute.[8] In David's time, when the nation had achieved some degree of stability, the king was free to launch aggressive action against his neighbors. The people of Moab and Edom, for example, "were treated with brutal severity. The Moabite fighting force was crippled by cold-blooded mass executions, and Moab made a vassal state tributary to David. Edom was likewise visited with frightful and systematic reprisals."[9]

The National Level

Centuries later, when the Israelite nation became well organized, oppressive structures developed within the nation itself. The oppression was the concerted work of the ruling class, which was made up of men of wealth and standing: leaders, subordinate officials, judges, prophets, and priests.[10] There were also, of course, prophets who were moved by the Spirit of Yahweh and who spoke out openly against injustice, pointing the finger at the oppressors.

In the Book of Psalms and elsewhere, the oppressor is spoken of as son of iniquity, enemy, adversary, haughty, impious, evildoer, proud, greedy. In short, oppressors are the *resha'im,* "the wicked," whose typical actions are violence, despoliation, deception, injustice.[11]

Rich women are also part of the oppressor class.[12] In the time of Amos, when Israel was not under any imperial yoke, the ruling classes grew rich and built magnificent palaces for themselves. They often gave great banquets; they bought costly furnishings for their homes. They derived profit even from worship and religion by means of its rituals and sacrifices. Amos attacks the wives of the powerful for thinking only of their great banquets. He compares them to the fat cows of Bashan, because they live the good life and are self-satisfied; it does not matter to them that they oppress *('ashaq)* the poor and crush *(ratsats)* the needy (Amos 4:1).

The Oppressed

The characteristics of the oppressed are exactly opposite those of the oppressor. They are poor; they have no social standing; the authorities pay no attention to them in the courts; and they have strong hope in God.

In the Old Testament the oppressed are called destitute, needy, innocent, suppliant, humble, unfortunate, or abandoned, depending on which of the several Hebrew words for "poor" is being used.[13] In a general way, the oppressed are the people of Yahweh: "What do you mean by crushing [*daka'*] my people, by grinding the face of the poor [*'ani*]?" (Isa. 3:15).

There are two interrelated reasons why the oppressed are always the poor: *they are oppressed because they are poor* (they have no means of subsistence, no power, and they live at the mercy of the oppressor); *they are poor because they are oppressed* (they are oppressed by being robbed and thus impoverished). A proverb shows the connection between poverty and oppression: "The poor man and the oppressor meet together; the Lord gives light to the eyes of both" (Prov. 29:13).

It is to be assumed that the opposite of "poor" is "rich" and that the opposite of "oppressor" is "oppressed." The text thus implies that oppressor and rich are synonyms, and that oppressed and poor are likewise synonyms.[14] We may therefore conclude that the oppressors are oppressors to the extent that they become rich, and that they are rich to the extent that they oppress the poor. Yahweh gives both the poor and the oppressor the opportunity to build a just society.[15]

Within the mass of the poor there are some who are doubly oppressed. In addition to being poor, they are also orphans or widows or resident aliens, and this state exposes them still further to the oppressor. The Mosaic law makes constant reference to these groups with a view to insuring their protection. The prophets, for their part, call special attention to the injustices done to them by the powerful. The three groups are utterly helpless: the orphans have no parents; the widows have no husbands; the resident aliens have no land or inheritance or family to give them backing in time of conflict (see Ps. 127:3–5), and in addition they live with foreigners.[16] In short, these are destitute people who are oppressed because they have no one to safeguard their rights.

Less frequently mentioned, but not therefore less important, are other groups that fall victim to oppression: day laborers, slaves, women,[17] and the prophets who denounce oppression.[18]

The love of Yahweh for his people and the love of the people for Yahweh make of all the oppressed a single body that experiences the death inflicted by exploitation. The Bible does not hesitate to speak of oppression as an action directed against Yahweh himself. In the final analysis, it is Yahweh who is oppressed: "If any one sins and commits a breach of faith against the Lord by deceiving his neighbor. . . or if he has oppressed his neighbor ['ashaq] . . ." (Lev. 6:2 [5:21]). "He who oppresses ['ashaq] a poor man insults his Maker, but he who is kind to the needy honors him" (Prov. 14:31; cf. Jer. 51:5).

The New Testament parable on the judgment of the nations (Matt. 25:31–46) expresses the same view of God. The support or rejection of God's "least," the poor, means glorifying or rejecting God.

The oppressed can be certain that their situation runs counter to Yahweh's will. The Psalms say as much in every verse. The oppressed are assured that "the joy of the godless is but for a moment" (Job 20:5); that things will change because Yahweh is just and defends all the oppressed ('ashaq; Ps. 103:6). The poor do not accept their condition; they know that the day will come when

> his [the oppressor's] children will seek the favor of the
> poor,
> and his hands will give back his wealth. . . .
> He swallows down riches and vomits them up again;
> God casts them out of his belly. . . .
> He will give back the fruit of his toil,
> and will not swallow it down;
> from the profit of his trading
> he will get no enjoyment [Job 20:10, 15, 18].

It is important to note that God hears and defends the cause of all the oppressed and not just of those who are oppressed in Israel.

The chastisement that the prophets foretell to the foreign nations is meant for the oppressors within these nations and not for the poor. Thus Yahweh says with regard to the Philistines: "The first-born of the poor will feed, and the needy lie down in safety; but I will kill your root with famine" (Isa. 14:30). And here is what he says in Jeremiah on the subject of Edom: " 'Leave your fatherless children, I will keep them alive; and let your widows trust in me.' For thus says the Lord: 'If those who did not deserve to drink the cup must drink it, will you go unpunished? You shall not go unpunished, but you must drink' " (Jer. 49:11–12).

Clearly, then, the vision of some of the biblical writers goes beyond Israel. It extends to all of the human race God's preferential love for the exploited peoples of the world.

NOTES

1. José Porfirio Miranda writes in *Marx and the Bible: A Critique of the Philosophy of Oppression*, trans. John Eagleson (Maryknoll, N.Y.: Orbis Books, 1974): "The philosophy of repression, perfected and refined through civilization as a true culture of injustice, does not achieve its greatest triumph when its propagandists knowingly inculcate it; rather the triumph is achieved when the philosophy has become so deeply rooted in the spirits of the oppressors themselves and their ideologues that they are not even aware of their guilt. Marx himself recognized that in the capitalist system the oppressor is as alienated as the oppressed" (p. xi).

2. Ps. 15 describes those who thus "dwell before the Lord."

3. Tomás Hanks, "La opresión y la pobreza en la teología bíblica," *Estudios Ecumenicos* 32/78 (Mexico City, CEE): 20.

4. See the oracles on the foreign nations in Isa. 13–35; Jer. 46–51.

5. Raúl Vidales, *Cristianismo Anti-burgués* (San José: DEI, 1978), pp. 116, 117.

6. Ibid., p. 117.

7. Among the books on the subject that I think most relevant to Latin America are John Bright, *A History of Israel*, 2nd ed. (Philadelphia: Westminster, 1972), which contains a detailed analysis of all these wars; and E. Cavaignac and P. Grelot, "The Historical Framework of the Bible," in A. Robert and A. Feuillet, eds., *Introduction to the Bible, 1: Old Testament,* trans. P. W. Skehan et

al. (New York: Desclee, 1968), pp. 5–69, where these various periods are surveyed.

8. Bright, *A History of Israel*, pp. 193–224. See also 2 Kings 11:15–18; 12:5; 2 Sam. 8:2; 12:31.

9. Ibid., pp. 197, 198–99.

10. See the scheming of which Ezek. 18–22 and Zeph. 2–3 speak.

11. See Miranda, *Marx and the Bible*, pp. 101–03, on the *resha'im* in Marx and the Bible. I emphasize this point because we often read of the "wicked" in the Psalms without realizing the full meaning of the word. Such words as "iniquitous," "impious," "proud" have a sociopolitical content that we usually overlook.

12. See Isa. 3:16–24; 32:9–14; Amos 4:1–3.

13. See Chapter 6, below.

14. The Hebrew text has *tok* in the plural. The translation of Reina and Valera has "usurer" for *tkakim*; in English, see, for example, JB.

15. The second half of the proverb should not be taken to mean that God is indifferent to the situation described. God's partiality for the poor and the needy is too evident in the Bible to allow such an interpretation. The verse is better taken as addressed to the poor; the intention of the saying appears to be to bring home to the poor that in human society all should have the same "light for their eyes," because God created a society in which equity was to reign. On the other hand, the rich too have an opportunity to build a just society if they cease to exploit others.

16. We should be clear in our minds on the type of foreigner whom the legal code protected. Israelite society distinguished three classes of foreigners: (1) foreign peoples, regarded as enemies (*zarim*); (2) foreigners resident in other countries but passing through Israel (*nakrim*), i.e., traders, visitors; (3) foreigners resident temporarily or permanently in Israel (*gerim*). The last named are the ones who are oppressed: the resident alien generally has no means of survival, cannot expect any inheritance, and "is also exposed to the caprice of his patron." See G. Stählin, "xenos," TDNT 5:8–10; K. G. Kuhn, "proselytos," TDNT 6:728–30. The quoted words are Kuhn's (6:728).

17. As a matter of fact, the oppression of women is rarely mentioned (Israelite society was patriarchal). Except for the oppression of the widow (who was oppressed not only as a woman but as a widow), there is barely a single text: Laban reminds Jacob not to make his wives, Leah and Rachel, feel inferior (*'anah*). All the other relevant texts refer to sexual violation and use *'anah* in the sense of "degrade, humiliate."

18. For example, Micaiah (1 Kings 22:17), Amos (Amos 7:12), Jeremiah (Jer. 18:18).

Chapter 4

Forms and Methods of Oppression

The oppressors are thieves and murderers, but their ultimate purpose is not to kill or impoverish the oppressed. Their primary objective is to increase their wealth at whatever cost.[1] The impoverishment and death of the oppressed are a secondary consequence.

In the methods used to achieve their goal, economic, ideological, and religious factors play their interrelated parts. Let us now consider in detail how the methods are applied in various situations of oppression; I shall again divide the material according to the two levels I have been considering.

The International Level

The Exodus story, better than any other section of the Bible, describes in a detailed and coherent way the manner in which the Israelites experienced oppression.

According to the text, the Egyptian empire had the entire Hebrew people under its power. A problem had arisen: the Hebrews had become "too many and too mighty for us [the Egyptians]" (Exod. 1:9). It was imperative, therefore, that some solution be found: "We must be prudent and take steps *against their increasing any further*, or if war should break out, they might add to the number of our enemies. They might take arms against us and so escape out of the country" (Exod. 1:10, JB).

The following methods of oppression then appeared:

41

The Enslavement and Exploitation of the Workers

"Therefore they set taskmasters over them to *afflict* [*'anah*] *them with heavy burdens*; and they built for Pharaoh store-cities, Pithom and Raamses" (Exod. 1:11). The word here used for "afflict," namely *'anah*, might well be translated as "enslave."

The means which the Egyptians took to prevent the departure (liberation) of the subject people consisted, in the first place, of "enslavement" through exploitation of the work force. The precautions taken by the Egyptians were supposed to have had three advantageous consequences:

1. the physical exhaustion of the Hebrews, which meant less frequent sexual relations and thus a slower rate of multiplication;

2. the dulling of the minds of the oppressed, so that the slaves would not think about their freedom (see Exod. 5:9);

3. the strengthening of the empire by means of the construction of the store-cities.

But the tactics failed, because "the more they were oppressed [*'anah*], the more they multiplied and the more they spread abroad" (Exod. 1:12).

The crisis in the empire became more acute; the Hebrews became a threat, and consequently the oppression and enslavement intensified: "The Egyptians *were in dread* of the people of Israel. So they made the people of Israel *serve with rigor*" (Exod. 1:12b–13).[2]

Genocide

The next step in Egyptian oppression was the murder of the children. The king gave the midwives the following order: "When you serve as midwife to the Hebrew women, and see them upon the birthstool, if it is a son, you shall *kill him*; but if it is a daughter, she shall live" (Exod. 1:16).

Again, the measure was fruitless, since the midwives did not obey the king's order. Pharaoh therefore ordered that every male child born to the Hebrews should be cast into the river (Exod. 1:22) and allowed to drown.

The Myth of Idleness

Here we have an ideological means of legitimizing oppression. When the first demand is made for the freedom of the Israelites (Exod. 5:1-3), Pharaoh answers the representatives of the enslaved people: "Moses and Aaron, why do you *take the people away from their work*" (5:4; cf. 5:5).[3] Pharaoh's reply to the demand is to intensify the exploitation (Exod. 5:6-10), in other words, to apply the first method even more rigorously.

In the view of the oppressor, the appeal for freedom, the celebration of a feast, and the whole idea of worship are simply lies and a cover for laziness: "They are *idle*; therefore they cry, 'Let us go and offer sacrifice to our God' " (Exod. 5:8). "Let heavier work be laid upon the men that they may labor at it and pay no regard to *lying words*" (5:9). "You are idle, you are idle; therefore you say, 'Let us go and sacrifice to the Lord.' Go now, and work; for no straw shall be given you, yet you shall deliver the same number of bricks" (5:17).

The Hebrew people in the service of the Egyptian empire became an object of hatred because they sought their freedom (5:22).

Deceitful Concessions

The Egyptian rulers realize that direct oppression is not working; in order, therefore, to defuse the crisis they grant certain requests of the Hebrews that are really peripheral. This method of maintaining a state of oppression is insidious because it evades and deflects the principal intention—complete freedom.

In the course of the ensuing struggle between Hebrews and Egyptians, Pharaoh keeps making concessions. None of these is accepted by the Hebrew leaders. Pharaoh can be seen to be yielding little by little, trying to avoid letting the enslaved people slip from his hands.

Pharaoh: "Go, sacrifice to your God *within the land*" (8:26).

Moses and Aaron: "It would not be right to do so. . . . We must go three days' journey into the wilderness and sacrifice to the Lord our God as he will command us" (8:26, 27).

Pharaoh: "I will let you go, to sacrifice to the Lord your God in the wilderness; *only you shall not go very far away*" (8:28).

No agreement is reached, and the struggle continues.

Pharaoh: "Who are to go?" (10:8).

Moses and Aaron: "We will go with our young and our old; we will go with our sons and daughters and with our flocks and herds, for we must hold a feast to the Lord" (10:9).

Pharaoh: "No! Go, *the men among you*, and serve the Lord, for that is what you desire" (10:11).

The struggle intensifies.

Pharaoh: "Go, serve the Lord; your children also may go with you; *only let your flocks and your herds remain behind*" (10:24).

Moses and Aaron: "Our cattle also must go with us; not a hoof shall be left behind, for we must take of them to serve the Lord our God" (10:26).

The struggle continues until the victory is won.

The Israelites refuse every offer made by the oppressor, and the oppressor cannot afford to yield any more. The dialogue breaks off (10:28–29); the confrontation intensifies and leads finally to the liberation of the enslaved people. If the Hebrews had accepted Pharaoh's concessions, the struggle would not have become increasingly radical and the Hebrews would not have gained their freedom.

Other oppressive situations in which the Hebrew people found themselves showed other styles of domination. The Hebrew words that most stand out at this level are *lahats* and *ratsats*, both of which contain the idea of "crushing."[4]

We will consider the various forms that the oppression takes.

The Meeting of Unequal Forces [5]

The ceaseless oppression (*lahats*, crush) suffered by the Hebrews in the period of the Judges is marked by the inequality of the confronting forces (inequality in weapons or number of fighting men): "He [Jabin] had nine hundred chariots of iron, and oppressed (*lahats*) the people of Israel cruelly for twenty years" (Judg. 4:3).[6]

Plunder and Slaughter

This method of oppression was common in all the wars described in the Old Testament.[7] It implied a crushing attack that brought death and desolation. Israel had been warned in the Covenant Code that if it did not obey the commandments the following would happen: "A nation which you have not known shall eat up the fruit of your ground and of all your labors; and you shall be only oppressed [*'ashaq*] and crushed [*ratsats*] continually" (Deut. 28:33).

This is precisely what happened on a number of occasions, as, for example, during the Midianite oppression:

> Whenever the Israelites put in seed the Midianites . . . would encamp against them and *destroy* the produce of the land . . . and *leave no sustenance* in Israel, and no sheep or ox or ass. For they would come up with their cattle and their tents, coming like locusts for number; both they and their camels could not be counted; so that they *wasted* the land as they came in. . . . And the people of Israel cried for help to the Lord [Judg. 6:3-6].

The Imposition of Tribute

During their periods of expansion, the various empires imposed heavy tribute on the different peoples they had conquered. Israel had to pay tribute to Egypt, Damascus, Assyria, Babylonia, and other nations that ruled them.[8] But Israel too, in its period of expansion, demanded tribute from other peoples (2 Sam. 8:2).

Exile

If an imperial power conquers a foreign people, plunders their land, imposes tribute on them, and this people continues to rebel, the empire endeavors to preserve its power by taking captives. That is, it sends those responsible for the rebellion into exile. The purpose of this drastic measure is to take from this people (Israel, Judah, or any other) any illusion of independence, to eradicate their native customs, and to destroy the sense of unity among persons of the same race, as well as to get free use of a labor force in building the empire's own cities.[9] The dominated nation is occupied by other peoples and its rulers are appointed by the empire or simply eliminated altogether.

Babylon took captive the people of Judah, and Assyria those of Israel: "Thus says the Lord of hosts: The people of Israel are oppressed [*'ashaq*], and the people of Judah with them; *all who took them captive* have held them fast, they refuse to let them go" (Jer. 50:33).

All these powerful nations that oppress Israel and Judah have their own gods and heap scorn on Yahweh. In the "Oracles against the Nations" (Jer. 46–51; Isa. 13–23), the prophets speak of these foreign nations as "arrogant," "haughty," or "proud."[10] Yahweh subdues and humbles them (*'anah*) when he takes vengeance on behalf of the oppressed (Isa. 25:5).

The National Level

The ruling class oppresses others more harshly when the country as a whole is not directly under the yoke of a foreign power.[11] The primary aim of this class is to accumulate wealth; the forms of oppression in which it indulges vary all the way from deception to murder.

Let us look at a straightforward and unequivocal example: the story of Naboth's vineyard (1 Kings 21). In this story the essential characteristics of an oppressor leap to the eye: he is rich and bent on accumulating even greater wealth; he has power because he is the king (Ahab), and the nobles are on his side; he is an idolater (1 Kings 21:26). In order to get what he wants (possession of Naboth's vineyard) he uses false testimony, his own power, and murder.

King Ahab says to Naboth: "Give me your vineyard, that I may have it for a vegetable garden, because it is near my house" (21:2). But Naboth refuses: "The Lord forbid that I should give you the inheritance of my fathers" (21:3).[12]

Jezebel, Ahab's wife, now enters the story. She says to the king: "Do you now govern Israel?" (21:7). She writes under the king's seal to the nobles and elders of the city and bids them set Naboth before the people with two false witnesses against him: "And let them bring a charge against him, saying, 'You have cursed God and the king.' Then take him out and stone him to death" (21:10).

That is what indeed happened: "They. . . set Naboth on high

among the people. And the two *base fellows* [i.e., false witnesses] came in and sat opposite him; and the base fellows brought a charge against Naboth. . . . So they took him outside the city, and stoned him to death" (21:12–13).

The king then took the vineyard for himself: "As soon as Ahab heard that Naboth was dead, Ahab arose to go down to the vineyard of Naboth, the Jezreelite, *to take possession of it*" (21:16).

According to this story, the oppressor is a thief, a man who abuses his authority, a murderer, and a liar.

In the sixth century B.C. Zephaniah in Judah attacks the injustices that are day by day turning the city into a place of death. Jerusalem, he says, is stained with the blood of the innocent; it is an oppressing [*'anah*] and rebellious city (Zeph. 3:1).

How is the oppression accomplished? Through the connivance of all the officials, who devour the people "like roaring lions" (Zeph. 3:3) and brutally oppress the weak. The judges twist the law and accept bribes, looking only to their own profit. The prophets approve these actions and fail to denounce oppression; and the priests violate God's laws that are meant for human benefit and profane what is holy (Zeph. 3:4).

Ezekiel, too, denounces Jerusalem, calling it "a city that sheds blood in the midst of her" (22:3). "In you men take bribes to shed blood; you take interest and increase and make gain of your neighbors by extortion [*'ashaq*]; and *you have forgotten me*, says the Lord God" (22:12).

There are common factors in these situations: the accumulation of possessions obtained through injustice; the power of the influential; idolatry and the abandonment of Yahweh.

Even if there is no obvious shedding of innocent blood, oppression is always deadly in its effects. Depending on the form used, oppression deprives (*gazal*) individuals of basic things they need in order to live: wages, clothing, food, and housing; it also deprives (*'anah*) them of their human dignity and their joyous response to life: the oppressed cannot sing as they used to (Ps. 137:4).

Behind almost all methods of oppression lies an *inversion of values*: people love evil and hate good (Mic. 3:2), but they call evil good and good evil: "Woe to those who call evil good and good evil, who put darkness for light and light for darkness, who put bitter for sweet and sweet for bitter!" (Isa. 5:20).

Over against this inversion of values Isaiah describes in messianic terms the government of the future king, who will oppose any oppression: "Behold, a king will reign in righteousness, and princes will rule in justice. . . . The fool will no more be called noble, nor the knave said to be honorable" (Isa. 32:1, 5). The fool will be a fool, and the noble a noble. Their actions will be seen by all and will be easily distinguishable.

The *fool* "speaks folly, and his mind plots iniquity. . . to utter error concerning the Lord, to leave the craving of the hungry unsatisfied, and to deprive the thirsty of drink. . . . He devises wicked devices to ruin the poor with lying words" (Isa. 32:6–7).

The *noble* person, however, "devises noble things, and by noble things he stands" (Isa. 32:8). "He who walks righteously and speaks uprightly, who despises the gain of oppressions, who shakes his hands, lest they hold a bribe . . ." (Isa. 33:15).

I shall analyze in detail the various methods and forms of oppression as practiced by the ruling class of Judah. In passing, I shall include other passages that are similar. I shall also cite the laws prohibiting the various forms of oppression.[13]

Exploitation of the Workers

In order to gain the maximum profit from production, the oppressor oppresses the workers, the day laborers. The oppressor obliges the day laborers to do excessive work and then holds back their pay. The Mosaic code contained clauses meant to protect such laborers: "You shall not oppress ['*ashaq*] a hired servant who is poor and needy, whether he is one of your brethren or one of the sojourners who are in your land within your towns; you shall give him his hire on the day he earns it, . . . [for he is poor and sets his heart upon it]" (Deut. 24:14–15).

And yet some of the nation's kings became great oppressors; Jehoiakim is an example. Here is Jeremiah's protest: "Woe to him who builds his house by unrighteousness, and his upper rooms by injustice; who makes his neighbor serve him for nothing, and does not give him his wages" (Jer. 22:13).

Slaves, too, were exploited. Israel had a reputation for treating slaves well, and as a result many slaves of other nations fled their masters and took refuge in Israel.[14] Nonetheless, to prevent their being oppressed there was a law: "You shall not give up to his master a slave who has escaped from his master to you; he shall dwell with you, in your midst, in the place which he shall choose within one of your towns, where it pleases him best; you shall not oppress him [*yanah*, enslave]" (Deut. 23:15–16).

This law orders the oppressor not to take advantage of the slave's situation, that is, to oppress him or to enter into any agreement with the slave's former master and oppressor. Persons become oppressors whether they exploit slaves themselves or return them to their former masters.

The resident alien (*ger*) was another common victim of this type of oppression (Ezek. 22:7). The law has this to say: "When a stranger sojourns with you in your land, you shall do him no wrong [*yanah*]. The stranger who sojourns with you shall be to you as the native among you, and you shall love him as yourself; for you were strangers in the land of Egypt" (Lev. 19:33–34).

Fraud

Fraud is a common method used by oppressors to enrich themselves. The fraud takes the form either of using false scales or engaging in deceitful transactions. "A trader [or: Canaanite], in whose hands are false balances, he loves to oppress [*'ashaq*]. Ephraim has said, 'Ah but I am rich, I have gained [deceitfully] wealth for myself' " (Hos. 12:7–8).

The law prohibits the use of false scales, but the oppressor breaks the law and commits fraud. The law is explicit: "You shall not have in your bag two kinds of weights, a large and a small. . . . A full and just weight you shall have. . . . For all who do such things, all who *act dishonestly*, are an abomination to the Lord your God" (Deut. 25:13–16).

And with regard to transactions the law says: "If you sell to your neighbor or buy from your neighbor, you shall not wrong [*yanah*, cheat] one another" (Lev. 25:14). The law goes on to say how buying and selling are to be done: "According to the number of years after the jubilee, you shall buy from your neighbor, and according to the number of years for crops he shall sell to you. If the years are many you shall increase the price, and if the years are few you shall diminish the price, for it is the number of crops that he is selling to you" (Lev. 25:15–16). This law assures equity in the transaction while at the same time resisting the monopolizing of land which Micah (2:2) denounces.[15]

Usury

The oppressor lends at interest because this is a way of making a very large profit. The Hebrew law expressly prohibits this: "If you lend money to any of my people with you who is poor, you shall not be to him as a creditor [or: usurer, JB], and you shall not exact interest from him (Exod. 22:25).

Ezekiel defines the upright person as one who practices right and justice, unlike the evildoer who "oppresses the poor and needy, . . . charges usury on loans and takes interest" (Ezek. 18:12–13, JB).

Jeremiah and Ezekiel attack the practice of usury in Israelite society as one of the crimes committed by Jerusalem (Jer. 22:17; Ezek. 22:7, 12).

Under this heading I must mention the pledge that a poor person must give in order to get the wherewithal to live. An oppressive moneylender usually takes and keeps the pledge. According to the law a widow's garment is not to be taken as a pledge (Deut. 24:17), nor is a mill or a millstone (Deut. 24:6). To take the latter "would be taking a life in pledge," since they are the tools the miller uses in gaining a livelihood. Moreover, when a pledge is offered, the lender is not to enter the neighbor's house and take the object pledged (originally a cloak); rather the one giving the pledge must bring it out. If the person offering the pledge is poor, the pledge must be returned in the evening so that the poor person will have a cloak for that night (Deut. 24:10–13; Exod. 22:26).

The prophet Habakkuk addresses oppressors in this way: "Woe to him who heaps up what is not his own . . . and loads himself with pledges!" (Hab. 2:6).

Bribery

Bribery is a form of oppression practiced by judges who take sides at the expense of the poor. Here is a proverb on oppression in the courts: "Do not rob the poor, because he is poor, or crush [*daka'*, pulverize] the afflicted at the gate [i.e., in the court]" (Prov. 22:22).

The function of judges, according to Deuteronomy, is as follows: "You shall not pervert justice; you shall not show partiality; and *you shall not take a bribe*, for a bribe blinds the eyes of the wise and subverts the cause of the righteous. Justice, and only justice, you shall follow" (Deut. 16:19–20).

But once oppression becomes institutionalized and permeates the entire social structure, judges become oppressors or connive with them: they "acquit the guilty for a bribe, and deprive the innocent of his right!" (Isa. 5:23). Zephaniah calls them "evening wolves that leave nothing till the morning" (Zeph. 3:3). Isaiah also accuses the rulers in Jerusalem: "Your princes are rebels and companions of thieves. Every one loves a *bribe* and runs after gifts. They do not defend the fatherless, and the widow's cause does not come to them" (Isa. 1:23).

The Oppressor Is Two-faced

Duplicity is an ideological way of hiding oppression and its agents. The oppressor does not engage openly in oppressive actions but goes about the matter subtly, by pretending to be devout or to stand by a friend. Yahweh has only reproach for this attitude of mind: "Behold, in the day of your *fast* you seek your own pleasure, and oppress [*nagash*] all your workers" (Isa. 58:3).

The oppressor conceals the fact of any responsibility, and the oppression simply happens, as it were. Psalm 55 explains: "His speech was smoother than butter, yet war was in his heart; his words were softer than oil, yet they were drawn swords" (Ps. 55:21). Psalm 10 presents the same idea: the oppressor is two-faced and does all that is possible to deceive the poor. "His eyes stealthily watch, . . . he lurks in secret, . . . he seizes the poor when he draws him into his net" (v. 8). And v. 7 says: "His mouth is filled with cursing and *deceit* and *oppression*; under his tongue are mischief and iniquity [*tok*].

Such is the tactic of this type of oppressor: "He devises wicked devices to ruin the poor man with lying words, even when the plea of the needy is right" (Isa. 32:7).

Murder

All the forms of evildoing I have listed directly affect the very life of the oppressed, since they take from the poor their means of livelihood and are thus deadly in their effects. Murder, the shedding of innocent blood, is simply undisguised killing.

The victims of the killing are the people of Yahweh: "They crush [*daka'*] thy people, O Lord, and afflict [*'anah*] thy heritage. They slay the widow and the sojourner, and murder the fatherless" (Ps. 94:5-6).

The following verses from Ezekiel show us how murderous oppression has for its background the desire to increase one's wealth. "Her princes . . . have devoured human lives; they have taken treasure and precious things; they *have made many widows* in the midst of her" (Ezek. 22:25). "Her princes . . . are like wolves tearing the prey, . . . *destroying lives* to get dishonest gain" (Ezek. 22:27).

Sexual Violation of Women

The term used for this act of oppression is *'anah*. In the texts I have been analyzing, this form of oppression is the only one not directly related to robbery or the accumulation of wealth. What does appear in many texts is a disparity of strength. The violater may be a prince who forces himself upon a virgin and then drives her from her home (2 Sam. 13:12-15). The violation may be so brutal that the woman dies, as in the case of the Levite's concubine: "The men of Gibeah rose against me. . . . They meant to kill me, and they *ravished* my concubine, and she *is dead*" (Judg. 20:5).

The law contains very detailed prescriptions with regard to rape.[16] For example: "If a man meets a virgin who is not betrothed, and seizes her and lies with her, and they are found, then the man who lay with her shall give to the father of the young woman fifty shekels of silver, and she shall be his wife, because he has violated [*'anah*] her; he may not put her away all his days" (Deut. 22:28-29). The next verse in the same passage prohibits incest.

The oppressor class in Israel ignores this law, and we find the prophet denouncing not only bribery and usury but rape as well: "In you they humble [*'anah*, do violence to] women who are unclean in their impurity [i.e., women who are menstruating]. One commits abomination with his neighbor's wife; another lewdly defiles his daughter-in-law; another in you defiles [*'anah*, does violence to] his sister, his father's daughter. . ." (Ezek. 22:10–11).

Let me summarize Part I. The analysis shows that oppression is historical in character and that the basic points of reference for understanding it are two identifiable and opposed groups. The oppressors are rich and influential people who never feel satisfied with what they have; their basic concern is to accumulate wealth. They turn to oppression and make use of various methods that bring them gain in one or another fashion. Oppressors are idolaters who follow false gods that can lend an aura of legitimacy to their actions; Yahweh, the God who demands that justice be done because he is himself justice and love, will not serve their purpose.

The oppressed are the impoverished, the slaves, the day laborers, the widows, the resident aliens, the orphans. All are poor and lack both social standing and power.

Oppression can occur between nations as well as within one and the same nation. The Hebrew people were initially oppressed by their Egyptian overlords. They were subjected to enslaving and degrading oppression, but after a struggle they attained their liberation.

The memory of this liberation was imprinted on the minds and hearts of the oppressed. At that time and in those circumstances they had experienced Yahweh. The law reminds them of those unforgettable events: "I am the Lord your God, who brought you out of the land of Egypt, out of the house of bondage" (Exod. 20:2). But the law also warns them against becoming oppressors in their turn: "You shall not wrong a stranger or oppress him, for you were strangers in the land of Egypt" (Exod. 22:21). Moreover, Yahweh identifies himself not only with "the chosen people" but with the oppressed populace as well, whether it is suffering slavery in Egypt (all of Israel) or suffering from the unjust actions of those Hebrews who are in a position of power.

As time passed after that first liberation and again after later liberations, Israel itself became an oppressor nation. More than that, its ambitious rulers and wealthy practiced oppression in its most wicked and deadly form: they piled up great riches for themselves and in the process multiplied the number of poor people, widows, and orphans: "They have devoured human lives; they have taken treasure and precious things; they have made many widows in the midst of her" (Ezek. 22:25).

The biblical narratives tell us that all oppressors (nations or groups within nations) were and always will be harshly punished for their oppression. Yahweh, the God who is faithful to the oppressed, takes vengeance on them. Thus Israel and Judah will be severely punished by other oppressors.

NOTES

1. We have already seen that *gazal,* "despoliation, robbery," is used with various words for oppression. See also the characteristic traits of the oppressor as sketched in Chapter 3.

2. See also Exod. 5:4–5; 6:6–18.

3. According to this whole passage (see 5:1), it is impossible to celebrate a feast and at the same time be a slave.

4. *'ashaq* also occurs (Exod. 28:33; Isa. 50:33; 52:4). Isaiah uses *nagash* in referring to the Babylonian tyrant in 14:2, 4.

5. See Judg. 4:3; 6:5; Isa. 22:6–8; Isa. 2:7.

6. When the Israelites were under the power of the king of Canaan they were frightened by the military strength used in oppressing them. Sisera, general of the army, was able to maintain and prolong his oppression because he had located his camp at a strategic point from which he controlled the entire plain of Esdraelon; see the remarks of F. Asensio, "Jueces," in *La Sagrada Escritura: Antiguo Testamento* (Madrid: BAC, 1968), 2:139.

7. Damascus: Isa. 17:14; Moab: Jer. 48:8, 32; Babylon: Isa. 14:17; 52:17–23; others: Jer. 49:1; Isa. 33:1, 4.

8. 2 Kings 12:18–19; 23:34; 18:14–15; Ezra 3:14.

9. The Second Book of Kings tells the story of the deportations; the prophets refer to them (Amos and Hosea refer to Assyria; Isaiah, Jeremiah, Micah, Zephaniah, Habakkuk, and Ezekiel refer to Babylon). On the political strategy of Tiglath-pileser, king of Assyria, see John Bright, *A History of Israel,* 2nd ed. (Philadelphia: Westminster, 1972), pp. 268–69; R. Wyatt, "Cautiverio," in W. Nelson, ed., *Diccionario Ilustrado de la Biblia* (Miami: Ed. Caribe, 1974), pp. 108–109.

10. Isa. 16:16; 23:7, 9; 13:11; 14:4; Jer. 48:29, 30, 42; 49:16.

11. Sometimes, however, the rulers oppressed the people because of the international situation, as, for example, when a tribute had been levied by a foreign power. Thus king Jehoiakim oppressed (*nagash*) his people by levying taxes in order to pay a tribute to Egypt (2 Kings 23:35).

12. "Inherited real estate bound the Israelite to his clan and was the basis of his rights as a citizen": Marciano Villanueva, "Samuel y Reyes," in *Biblia de Jerusalén* (1975), p. 393.

13. Since I shall be citing various laws, it is important to keep in mind the original intent of these Hebrew laws (originally called *mishpatim*: Exod. 21:1), which is that the rights of the poor be protected and that justice be done to them. This is why the psalmist says: "For all thy commandments are justice" (Ps. 119:172). According to José Porfirio Miranda "the only meaning of the law is to do justice in the strictest and most social sense" (*Marx and the Bible: A Critique of the Philosophy of Oppression,* trans. John Eagleson [Maryknoll, N.Y.: Orbis Books, 1974], p. 151). In the New Testament Paul attacks a law that has been mythologized and, instead of providing guidelines for living, has become an instrument of oppression and sin. Acccording to Miranda there is no difference between the "justice of God" in Paul and the meaning which "the law" has in the Psalms. He adds: "Paul's revolutionary and absolutely central message that justice has been achieved without the law, would lack all force if this were not precisely the same justice that the law hoped to realize. This is the revolutionary and unprecedented core of his message" (*Marx and the Bible*, p. 152).

14. See R. Criado, "Deuteronomio," in *La Sagrada Escritura: Antiguo Testamento* (Madrid: BAC, 1977), 1:901.

15. Manuel Revuelta, "Ezequiel, Daniel y Profetas Menores," in *Biblia de Jerusalén* (1975), p. 1,336.

16. Deut. 22:24, 29; 21:14.

PART II

THE GOOD NEWS
OF LIBERATION

Everyone knows that the gospel proclaims life. Jesus said: "I came that they may have life, and have it abundantly" (John 10:10). Yet in Latin America people experience only poverty, misery, death. Where, then, is this life?

Everyone knows, too, that the gospel preaches love: "He who does not love his brother. . . cannot love God" (1 John 4:20). Yet oppression and exploitation are to be seen all around us. Where, then, is this love?

The gospel proclaims freedom: "The truth will make you free" (John 8:32). But among our peoples there is only repression. Where, then, is this freedom?

Where are the life, the love, the freedom that the gospel proclaims?

Clearly, something has gone awry in the reading of God's word. *Struggle, life,* and *liberation* have been replaced by *passivity, resignation,* and *submission.* In other words, the gospel has been reduced to a set of individualistic terms relating only to the "spiritual" order.

In Part II I want to present another way of reading the Bible, a way that will encourage the ambitions and desires of the people, stimulate them to live their lives more fully, and discredit a reading that leads to death.

When the Bible is read in a context of oppression, such as exists in Latin America, and with a view to freeing men and women from this oppression, it has much to say to us.

Chapter 5, "God and Liberation," seemed appropriate inasmuch as liberation and oppression are correlative terms and, as I state at the beginning, the oppression-liberation theme is at the heart of biblical faith. In addition, it is extremely important in our day to understand the concept which the oppressed Hebrew people had of God as their liberator.

Chapter 6 has to do with the good news of hope and life for the masses. Chapter 7 suggests a way of understanding "conversion": as a first step toward struggle and the affirmation of human life.

Chapter 5

God and Liberation

Liberation is an important part of the structure of the biblical narratives that report oppressive situations. Oppression and liberation are at once correlative and in conflict with each other. I call them "correlative" because liberation is possible only when there is oppression; oppression is a condition for liberation. They are in conflict because one is sin and the other salvation, and the transition from the one to the other requires a struggle between the forces that seek to continue the oppression and the forces that seek freedom. From the viewpoint of semantics "liberation" is "a word of confrontation and conflict."[1]

There are, then, three different phases in the structure of the texts I have analyzed in Part I (the phases may be actually present or only anticipated by the prophets): oppression, liberation, and a new and just order.

The Essence of Freedom

I have described in detail those who cause oppression, those who suffer it, and the various forms and methods of oppression. I have also given a concrete analysis of what is involved in the act of oppressing. I think it is also important to indicate, on the basis of my analysis, what is basically involved in a "life of freedom."

To begin with, this freedom has nothing to do with the liberal ideology that talks so glibly of the right to freedom. "Freedom," in the present context, means essentially the actual recovery of those basic necessities that the oppressor has taken from the poor: their land (Lev. 25), the wages of the day laborer (Jer.

22:13), the object given as a pledge (usually the blanket with which people cover themselves) (Hab. 2:6), their dwellings (Job 20:19), and their human dignity (cf. *'anah*).

On the one hand, then, the injustice that marks situations of oppression is to be seen in:

> the accumulation of wealth stolen from the poor (their
>   land, wages, food, houses, pledges)
> the powerlessness of the poor
> idolatry
> unjust administration of authority
> degradation of the oppressed
> violence
> death
> subjection
> deception, lies
> suffering

On the other hand, the justice that marks a free life finds expression in:

> an equitable distribution of possessions and power and,
>   with it, the elimination of poverty
> the presence of God
> just government
> humanization
> peace
> life
> freedom
> truth
> joy

Liberation (i.e., the action of liberating) implies a tenacious and unceasing struggle. It is important for us to ask at this point who the liberator is of whom the Old Testament speaks.

The Historical Liberator

The narratives of the Old Testament attribute every act of liberation to Yahweh. For example, in the literary genre of "stories which have wars as their subject,"[2] God is spoken of as the one who throughout history fights wrathfully in defense of the oppressed. We find metaphors such as this one: "The Lord is riding on a swift cloud," headed for Egypt (Isa. 19:1).

If we take the stories literally, we must conclude that Yahweh's intervention is so overpowering as to eliminate any human participation and to make the victories completely miraculous.

But other stories (those in Judges, for example) describe the struggle as involving the oppressed people, even though the victory is attributed to Yahweh. The people act and, since Yahweh is with them in the struggle, they gain the victory (Judg. 6:16; 8:1).

In the minds of many, these two ways of conceiving the struggle give rise to the problem of the historical agent of liberation: Is it the people? Is it Yahweh?

In the light of a serious and comprehensive reading of the Old Testament I offer the following interpretation.

In situations of oppression the oppressed and Yahweh meet and join forces. The one cries out *(sa'aq)* and the Other listens and heeds *(shama')*; then the one learns that the Other has listened and heeded the cry (Exod. 4:31). Both listen to one another, and both struggle as though they were a single person, because the enemies of the oppressed are also the enemies of God (Judg. 5:31).

In the Bible the historical agent of liberation is Yahweh acting through the oppressed; at the same time it is the oppressed who determine that they will no longer yield to the oppressor and who are fully convinced that God, Yahweh, gives them strength enough to win the victory. They know that without this God the battle is lost. All the factors that favor liberation are felt by the oppressed to be signs of the presence of Yahweh.

We read in the Bible that liberation is always connected with the experience of God.[3] And the intensity of the vision is such that the very struggle turns into a profession of faith rather than a simple military engagement.[4]

It is not to be thought that Yahweh literally *takes the place* of the oppressed in their historical struggle. Such a view could have negative consequences such as the abandonment of all human effort in the expectation that Yahweh, when called upon, will "intervene." All this means that in our present historical situation of oppression/liberation, our faith in the God of the Bible does not excuse us from taking part in the struggle for liberation. As José Míguez Bonino says, we have the power to transform and recreate the world materially. And God is with us, "but he does not make us superfluous."

> The world is the space given to human beings where they may be themselves. God will answer their call, share their struggles, suffer and rejoice with them. But God does not invade their space nor turn it into something to be manipulated. . . . Jesus Christ did not come to be a substitute for human beings but rather to open for them the way by which they can accomplish their human task.[5]

If we are to grasp in a Christian perspective the special nature of the historical agent of liberation, it is important that we take into account the language of the Bible and the conception of God which the oppressed people have.

Who Is Yahweh to the Oppressed?

The Bible is a book of testimonies. God is experienced in a vital way; he does not make himself known in a purely intellectual manner.[6] The "creed" of the Hebrews speaks primarily of the events they have lived through: events which bear witness to Yahweh as a just and liberating God (Deut. 26:5–10).

Yahweh concretizes in himself the justice and love that are experienced in the course of history. And since justice and love cannot become concrete realities except in a society where there is no oppression, Yahweh comes on the scene at every moment in solidarity with the oppressed, for the purpose of assuring the concrete realization of love and the removal of oppressors.

The Israelites conceived of Yahweh as the God who called them and required that they follow the paths of justice which were traced out for them in the law.[7] This is why we so often come across such phrases as "seek justice," "do good," and "free the oppressed from the hands of the oppressor." For the Israelite people Yahweh is the one who sees to the fulfillment of the law. Many laws take some such form as this: "You shall not wrong one another, but you shall fear your God; for I am the

Lord your God" (Lev. 25:17). "You shall not afflict any widow
or orphan. If you do afflict them, and they cry out to me, I will
surely hear their cry, and my wrath will burn, and I will kill you
with the sword" (Exod. 22:23–24). "I will be a swift witness . . .
against those who oppress the hireling in his wages, the widow
and the orphan, against those who thrust aside the sojourner,
and do not fear me, says the Lord of hosts" (Mal. 3:5).

In the Israelite view Yahweh is the manifestation of justice.
The terms *tsedeq* (justice, righteousness), *mishpat* (right,
judgment), *hesed* (mercy, steadfast love), and *'emet* (truth,
fidelity) define his presence.[8] The people sing to him: "Justice
and right are the foundation of thy throne; mercy and truth go
before thee" (Ps. 89:14).

The following text shows how Yahweh and *mishpat–tsedeq* are
set in parallel: "For Yahweh has not abandoned or deserted his
hereditary people; for judgment [*mishpat*] will return to justice
[*tsedeq*], and, in its wake, all upright hearts" (Ps. 94:14–15).

The "justice" of God is not an attribute which human beings
have predicated of him, but rather refers to the historical self-
revelation of God in experiences of justice and in his fidelity to
the community.[9]

The oppressed people, for their part, feel that in their efforts
and in their way of life Yahweh gives them power and is with
them, because these efforts and this way of life are directed to
the concretization of love. There is a fusion of God and his
people. The people struggle by the power and strength of God,
because God is a liberator. Here is how the Psalms speak of him:

> Our God is a God of salvation;
>> and to God, the Lord, belongs escape from death.
> The God of Israel . . . gives power and strength to his
>> people.
> Blessed be God! [Ps. 68:20, 35].

> Blessed are the people who know the festal shout,
>> who walk, O Lord, in the light of thy countenance,
> who exult in thy name all the day,
>> and extol thy justice.
> For thou art the glory of their strength;
>> by thy favor our horn is exalted [Ps. 89:15–17].

. . . My hand shall ever abide with him,
   my arm also shall strengthen him.
The enemy shall not outwit him,
   the wicked shall not humble him.
I will crush his foes before him
   and strike down those who hate him [Ps. 89:21–23].

But even if there is no distinction between the people's struggle
and the divine action, Yahweh does retain his own identity, and
this is due to the fact that God always shows himself and will
continue to show himself as calling for the concretization of
love. He will always be "the horizon that is open to creativity
and historical initiative."[10] He will be "the one who summons us
onward by reminding us of our vocation to transform nature
and create a just world."[11] Anyone who does not meet the demand, who does not follow in his ways, will be unfaithful to this
God:

Love and truth will meet;
   justice and peace will kiss each other.
Truth will spring up from the ground,
   and justice will look down from the sky.

Yea, the Lord will give what is good,
   and our land will yield its increase.
Justice will go before him,
   and make his footsteps a way [Ps. 85:11–13].

NOTES

1. Hugo Assmann, *Opresión-Liberación: Desafío a los Cristianos* (Montevi-
deo: Tierra Nueva, 1971), p. 38; English translation in Assmann's *Theology for a
Nomad Church,* trans. Paul Burns (Maryknoll, N.Y.: Orbis Books, 1976), p. 47.

2. Gerhard von Rad, *Old Testament Theology,* trans. D. M. G. Stalker, 2
vols. (New York: Harper and Row, 1962–65), 2:378–79.

3. See Pablo Richard, *Cristianismo, lucha ideológica, y racionalidad so-
cialista* (Salamanca: Ed. Sígueme, 1975): "It is within the political struggle for
liberation that the Israelite people experiences God" (p. 67).

4. Von Rad, *Old Testament Theology,* 2:379.

5. José Míguez Bonino, *Espacio por los hombres* (Buenos Aires: Tierra Nueva, 1975), p. 23; Eng. trans. *Room to Be People* (Philadelphia: Fortress, 1979).

6. The same can be said of our base-level ecclesial communities. "They have no intellectual definition of God. For them God is as concrete a task and as much identified with their lives as the experience of love and the experience of the struggle" (Frei Betto, "Dios brota en la experiencia de la vida," in *La lucha de los Dioses* [San José, Costa Rica: Departamento Ecuménico de Investigaciones; Managua, Nicaragua: Centro Antonio Valdivieso, 1980], p. 193; to be published in English by Orbis Books as *The Battle of the Gods*).

7. On the notion of "law" see n. 13 of Chapter 4, above.

8. In the rest of this chapter we follow the translation of these terms as suggested by José Porfirio Miranda, *Marx and the Bible,* trans. John Eagleson (Maryknoll, N.Y.: Orbis Books, 1974).

9. The concept of God's justice as a divine attribute originates in Greek philosophy with its speculation on the divine attributes. See Ernst Käsemann, "Gottesgerechtigkeit bei Paulus," in his *Exegetische Versuche und Besinnungen* 2, 3rd ed. (Göttingen: Vandenhoeck und Ruprecht, 1970), pp. 186–87.

10. Victorio Araya, "El Dios de la Alianza . . . Estratégica," in *La lucha de los Dioses,* p. 131.

11. Ibid.

Chapter 6

Good News for the Poor

*I bring you good news
of a great joy which will come
to all the people [Luke 2:10].*

In the first century A.D. the ordinary people of Palestine
found themselves in extremely difficult circumstances. Like all
Jews they had to pay heavy taxes to the Roman Empire; in addition, they suffered greatly from the inflation that was prevalent
from Egypt to Syria. In the cities there was growing unemployment, and slavery was on the increase. For these reasons, slaves
and farm workers abandoned their places and formed robber
bands to prey on the caravans of traders and pilgrims.[1]

Meanwhile, there was another social class that did not suffer
from this situation but, on the contrary, possessed economic and
political power in Palestine and profited from inflation. These
were the people who formed the council of elders (generally, men
from the noble and powerful families), the chief priests, the
great landowners, the rich merchants, and others who exercised
some political and ideological control (the scribes, Pharisees,
Sadducees). This class collaborated with the Roman Empire and
acted in ways hostile to the masses of the people. Its members
were the open enemies of the Zealots, a guerrilla group that
wanted to take power and drive out the Romans.[2]

It was in this historical context that the Good News came.

In Latin America there are also great masses of people who
live in extremely difficult circumstances. Inflation is a very serious problem in almost all the countries of this part of the Third
World, and it is evident that its effects bear most heavily on the
masses, that is, the poor.

Other serious problems the poor have to face are unemployment, lack of housing, malnutrition, extreme indigence, exploitation.

On the other hand, there is a group that is small by comparison with the population as a whole, but that nonetheless has great economic and political power. Some in this group exploit the proletariat in order to accumulate capital; others derive great profit by becoming partners in foreign companies or by enabling the latter to operate freely in Latin America.

The ruling class, as in first-century Palestine, collaborates in the expansion of the wealthy nations. Latin American countries governed by the military receive weapons from abroad in order to put down the discontented masses. In some Latin American countries governments favor the entrance of the multinational corporations on the pretext that this will foster industrial development.

At the international level, the economies of the Latin American countries are dependent on foreign nations and are structured according to the interests of the wealthy nations of the world. As everyone knows, these nations see Latin America as a source of raw material and cheap labor.

In such a situation the poor feel oppressed; they are hard put to breathe and stay alive. Extreme poverty and exploitation are killing them. They are forced to rise up and fight for the life of the masses.

At this moment in history good news is urgently needed.

The Good News

The Good News takes a very concrete form. The central message is this: the situation cannot continue as it is; impoverishment and exploitation are not God's will; but now there is hope, resurrection, life, change. The reign of God, which is the reign of justice, is at hand.

We have often been told that the message contained in the Good News is that Christ came into the world to save us or free us from sin. But sin is identified with those actions that society considers immoral; drug taking, adultery, excessive drinking, and so on. Thus the gospel of life is reduced to a simple behavioral change.

But the Good News cannot be so reduced. After all, any non-Christian religion can propose that kind of moral teaching, which amounts to nothing but a set of patches designed to cover over the great sin that lies underneath: oppression at the national and international, the individual and collective levels.

The message of the Good News is of the liberation of human beings from everything and everyone that keeps them enslaved. That is why the Good News brings joy and hope.

Mary, the humble mother of Jesus, sang this song when she visited her cousin Elizabeth:

> My soul magnifies the Lord,
> and my spirit rejoices in God my Savior,
> for he has regarded the low estate of his handmaiden. . . .
> He has shown strength with his arm,
> he has scattered the proud in the imagination of their
>   hearts,
> he has put down the mighty from their thrones,
> and exalted those of low degree;
> he has filled the hungry with good things,
> and the rich he has sent empty away. . .[Luke 1:46–53].

Mary is here speaking not of individuals undergoing moral change but of the restructuring of the order in which there are rich and poor, mighty and lowly (vv. 52–53).

The priest Zechariah likewise saw the Good News as the fulfillment of the promise of liberation:

> Blessed be the Lord God of Israel,
> for he has visited and redeemed his people,
> and has raised up a horn of salvation for us . . . ,
> as he spoke by the mouth of his holy prophets from of old,
> that *we should be saved from our enemies,*
> *and from the hand of all who hate us* [Luke 1:68–71].

The news is therefore good news to the people; it is a reason for joy and gladness, since it gives the hope of a total change. In Luke 2:10 a messenger of the Lord tells the shepherds: "I bring you good news of a great joy which will come to all the people."

The Good News is evidently not so good for some people.

King Herod was deeply concerned when they told him that the king of the Jews had been born. We are told that because he feared to lose his throne he ordered the killing of all children in Bethlehem who were less than two years old (Matt. 2:16).

The shepherds, on the other hand, rejoiced when they heard the News. The shepherds were men who lived in the fields and took turns watching over their flocks at night (Luke 2:10). They enjoyed little respect because they were part of the masses. When they received the Good News, they were glad; they listened to it and shared it with others.

The Good News that speaks of the liberation of the oppressed cannot be pleasing to the oppressors, who want to go on exploiting the poor. But the Good News is indeed good to those who want to change and to see a more just society.

For the most part, those who want to live in a society in which justice and peace reign are those who suffer hunger, oppression, poverty. For this reason the Good News is directed especially to the poor. Jesus himself said so when he read from the Book of Isaiah:

> The Spirit of the Lord is upon me,
> because he has anointed me
> to *preach good news to the poor.*
> He has sent me to proclaim release to the captives
> and recovering of sight to the blind,
> to set at liberty those who are oppressed,
> to proclaim the acceptable year of the Lord.
> [Luke 4:18–19]

Then he added: "Today this scripture has been fulfilled in your hearing" (Luke 4:21).

The Poor

Knowing, then, that the Good News is addressed especially to the poor, let us reflect on who the poor are and why they are poor.

For many centuries now the biblical passages on the poor have been spiritualized and distorted. Poverty is regarded as a virtue, as an abstract quality that can be attributed to rich and poor alike. As a result, a rich person can be understood to be poor "in spirit," and a poor person rich "in spirit."

The beatitudes that Jesus addressed to the poor have been read as referring to something spiritual. In this distorted view, the "poor in spirit" may be:

1. those who have accepted (material) poverty voluntarily and without protest;

2. those who, though rich, are not proud but rather act humbly before God and their fellows (neither the riches nor the way they have been acquired are an *obstacle* to acting humbly);

3. those who are restless spirits and lack any element of the mystical in their religious outlook.

And yet, when Jesus reads the promise now fulfilled in him: "He anointed me to preach good news to the poor," he is referring to all those who lack the basic necessities of life. When he says: "Blessed are you poor" (Luke 6:20), he is referring to material poverty. The poor in spirit are the "poor of Yahweh," that is, they are the poor and oppressed who acknowledge their poverty, and who stand before God as poor people. In other words, they are not the kind of poor people who think, and try to live, as members of the bourgeoisie.

To sum up: the poor in the Bible are the helpless, the indigent, the hungry, the oppressed, the needy, the humiliated. And it is not nature that has put them in this situation; they have been unjustly impoverished and despoiled by the powerful.

In the Old Testament there are a number of Hebrew words that are often translated by "poor":[3]

1. *'ani* in its most fully developed use describes a situation of inferiority in relation to another. Concretely the *'ani* is one who is dependent. When used in combination with *dal* it describes an economic relationship. The contrary of the *'ani* is the oppressor or user of violence. God is protector of the *'anim* because they are people who have been impoverished through injustice;

2. *dal* is used in two senses: it may refer either to physical weakness or to a lowly, insignificant position in society;

3. *'ebion* often refers to those who are very poor and in a wretched state. Originally it meant someone who asks for alms, a beggar;

4. *rash* is the poor or needy person; its antithesis is the rich

person. The social and economic meaning is the prominent one;
    5. *misken* means "dependent," a social inferior.

I have listed these Hebrew words with their connotations in
order to show that according to almost all of them the poor are
individuals who are inferior to the rich or the powerful. Their
situation is not the result of chance but is due to the action of
oppressors. This point is brought out in many passages of the
Bible: "They sell the righteous for silver, and the needy for a pair
of shoes—they that trample the head of the poor into the dust of
the earth, and turn aside the way of the afflicted" (Amos 2:6–7);
"The people of the land [or: the landowners] have practiced
extortion and committed robbery; they have oppressed the poor
and needy, and have extorted from the sojourner without redress" (Ezek. 22:29).

There is evidently no need to reread the entire Bible in order to
discover that poor persons are those who do not have the wherewithal to live because their means have been snatched away.

The authorities, for their part, frequently prove to be on the
side of injustice. They close their eyes to the sinful activities of
the powerful, and their role is, in fact, to maintain this order of
things. Isaiah denounces them: "Your princes are rebels and
companions of thieves. . . . They do not defend the fatherless,
and the widow's cause does not come to them" (Isa. 1:23).

Orphans and widows were listed among the poor and helpless,
because they had no one to defend them and no means of subsistence.

The accumulation of wealth is incompatible with Christianity,
since any accumulation of possessions is at the cost of the very
poor. The denunciation pronounced by Jeremiah is very clear:
"Woe to him who builds his house by unrighteousness, and his
upper rooms by injustice; who makes his neighbor serve him for
nothing, and does not give him his wages" (Jer. 22:13).

The New Testament also launches a strong attack on those
who heap up possessions:

Come now, you rich, weep and howl for the miseries that
are coming upon you. Your riches [i.e., hoards] have rotted
and your garments are moth-eaten. Your gold and silver
have rusted, and their rust will be evidence against you and

you will eat your flesh like fire. You have laid up treasure
for the last days. Behold, the wages of the laborers who
mowed your fields, which you kept back by fraud, cry out;
and the cries of the harvesters have reached the ears of the
Lord of hosts. You have lived on the earth in luxury and in
pleasure; you have fattened your hearts in a day of slaugh-
ter. You have condemned, you have killed the righteous
man; he does not resist you [James 5:1-6].

At this point we are in a position to infer two points about the
poor as seen by the Bible. First, poverty is regarded as something
decidedly negative; it is "a scandalous condition" and the manifestation of "a degrading human condition."[4] Secondly, this
situation of poverty is not the result of some historical inevitabil-
ity nor is it "just the way things are"; it is, as we saw in Part I,
the result of the unjust actions of oppressors.[5]

Blessed Are the Poor

God, of course, is not indifferent toward situations of injustice. God takes sides and comes on the scene as one who favors
the poor, those who make up the masses of the people. The Bible
makes perfectly clear this divine predilection and option for the
poor.

The poor alone are worthy to take part in the kingdom of
God. Unless the rich break with their way of life, they cannot
enter this kingdom. Zacchaeus, who was a chief tax collector
and a very rich man, had to give half of his goods to the poor
and pay a fourfold recompense to those he had exploited. We see
a quite different response in the case of the rich young man
whom Christ calls: he has the opportunity to share in the
kingdom of God, but since he cannot detach himself from his
possessions and give them to the poor, there is no place for him
in the kingdom. With reason does Christ say: "Truly, I say to
you, it will be hard for a rich man to enter the kingdom of
heaven. Again I tell you, it is easier for a camel to go through the
eye of a needle than for a rich man to enter the kingdom of
God" (Matt. 19:23-24).

In Chapter 6 of Luke's Gospel we find contrasting but parallel
statements that are part of Jesus' teachings to his followers:

Blessed are you poor, for yours is the kingdom of God [v. 20].
> But woe to you that are rich, for you have received your consolation [v. 24].

Blessed are you, that hunger now, for you shall be satisfied [v. 21].
> Woe to you that are full now, for you shall hunger [v. 25].

Blessed are you that weep now, for you shall laugh [v. 21].
> Woe to you that laugh now, for you shall mourn and weep [v. 25].

The reason why the Bible opposes the rich is not because they are rich, but because they have acquired their riches at the expense of their neighbors (James 5:1-6).

Chapter 5 of Matthew's Gospel contains further beatitudes for the poor:

Blessed are the poor in spirit, for theirs is the kingdom of heaven.
Blessed are those who mourn, for they shall be comforted.
Blessed are the meek, for they shall inherit the earth.
Blessed are those who hunger and thirst for righteousness, for they shall be satisfied.
Blessed are the merciful, for they shall obtain mercy.
Blessed are the pure in heart, for they shall see God.
Blessed are the peacemakers, for they shall be called sons of God.
Blessed are those who are persecuted for righteousness' sake, for theirs is the kingdom of heaven [Matt. 5:3-10].

God identifies himself with the poor to such an extent that their rights become the rights of God himself: "he who oppresses a poor man insults his Maker, but he who is kind to the needy honors him" (Prov. 14:31); "he who mocks the poor insults his Maker; he who is glad at calamity will not go unpunished" (Prov. 17:5).

It is clear that these many passages of the Bible in favor of the poor are in serious danger of being subjected to another kind of spiritualization: that of calling upon the poor to be satisfied with their state, not of poverty as such, but of privilege in God's sight. This would be disastrous because then even the rich would feel tempted to experience certain wants in order that they too might be God's favorites. Then the situation of injustice that God condemns would be alleviated in the eyes of the world.

We must always keep in mind, therefore, that poverty is an unworthy state that must be changed. I repeat: poverty is not a virtue but an evil that reflects the socioeconomic conditions of inequality in which people live. Poverty is a challenge to God the Creator; because of the insufferable conditions under which the poor live, God is obliged to fight at their side.

In Latin America the poor are blessed, but the reason is not that they have resigned themselves to poverty but, on the contrary, that they cry out and struggle and have their mouths shut for them on the grounds that "they are rebels and have recourse to violence." They are blessed, but not because they voluntarily seek to be poor, for it is the mode of production forced upon Latin America that leads them to penury. They are blessed, but not because they have scorned riches; on the contrary, it is they themselves who have been scorned by those who monopolize the world's riches.

The poor in Latin America are blessed because the reign of God is at hand and because the eschatological promise of justice is drawing ever nearer to fulfillment and, with it, the end of poverty.

NOTES

1. Fernando Belo, *Uma Leitura Política do Evangelho* (Lisbon: Multinova, 1974), p. 43. In English see Belo's *A Materialistic Reading of the Gospel of Mark*, trans. Matthew J. O'Connell (Maryknoll, N.Y.: Orbis Books, 1981).

2. Ibid., pp. 37 and 44.

3. Julio de Santa Ana, *Good News to the Poor: The Challenge of the Poor in the History of the Church*, trans. Helen Whittle (Maryknoll, N.Y.: Orbis Books, 1979), p. 10, n. 1.

4. Gustavo Gutiérrez, *A Theology of Liberation: History, Politics and Salvation*, trans. Sister Caridad Inda and John Eagleson (Maryknoll, N.Y.: Orbis Books, 1973), pp. 291–92.

5. Ibid., pp. 292–93.

Chapter 7

Conversion as an Affirmation of Life

You recently repented and did what is right in my eyes by proclaiming liberty, each to his neighbor [Jer. 34:15].

It is said that our Latin American peoples are eminently Christian. It has even been said that Christianity is an intrinsic component of Latin America.

But the statement is a contradiction, because, while the gospel preaches life, justice, and freedom, the masses of our peoples live in abject poverty and are oppressed and repressed.

To a great extent, this contradictory situation is due to the fact that Latin America has not experienced a genuine *conversion*.

For many years we have been taught that conversion consists simply in believing in Jesus Christ. But an analysis of the biblical data on conversion shows it to be an experience that far transcends an act of belief.

Let us look at the detailed evidence for this statement.

The Idea of Conversion

The koine Greek word *metanoia* has been translated in various versions of the Bible as conversion, repentance, correction, change of attitude, and so on. But none of these words really puts a finger on what the term *metanoia* properly means. In fact, it is rather difficult to express the full meaning of the term in a single English word.

Conversion *(metanoia)* means a radical change of outlook

that must show itself in concrete acts of justice. It means a total transformation of the person; a rebirth accompanied by an "unlimited willingness"[1] to engage in action.

In the New Testament the idea expressed in *metanoia* is not derived either from its lexical meaning or from its usage in classical Greek.[2] If we are to analyze the word accurately we must have recourse to Hebrew thought. When Jews spoke of *metanoia* they had in mind the Hebrew root *shub,* which, in most cases, meant "to turn around," "to return," "to be converted." A person turned to God and turned away from evil, evil actions, violence, idols; in a word, from sin in all its forms.

In the Old Testament the element of repentance or remorse found various external expressions: sacrifices, fasting, the wearing of sackcloth, and so on. The prophets were harsh in their criticism of these expressions of penance because they did not imply a real conversion. The Israelites hoped to please God by such actions, but God answered them:

> Is such the fast that I choose,
> a day for a man to humble himself?
> Is it to bow down his head like a rush,
> and to spread sackcloth and ashes under him?
> Will you call this a fast,
> and a day acceptable to the Lord?
> Is not this the fast that I choose:
>> to loose the bonds of wickedness,
>> to undo the thongs of the yoke,
>> to let the oppressed go free,
>> and to break every yoke?
> Is it not to share your bread with the hungry,
> and bring the homeless poor into your house;
> when you see the naked, to cover him,
> and not to hide yourself from your own flesh?
> Then . . . your righteousness shall go before you,
> the glory of the Lord shall be your rear guard. . . .
> And the Lord . . . will make your bones strong.
>   [Isa. 58:5–11]

It is not enough to feel remorse of conscience for what has been done or omitted, and to confess one's sin in order to gain forgiveness. The important thing is a sincere conversion, or turning to God, and this implies all that we have just heard the prophet Isaiah calling for in God's name. Conversion, therefore, must include a repentance that leads to a new manner of life and to just actions: "But if a wicked man turns away from all his sins which he has committed and keeps all my statutes and does what is lawful and right, he shall surely live" (Ezek. 18:21).

To turn to God, to be converted, means to act in the ways that please God. And the following verses tell us just what it is that pleases God: "You recently repented and did what was right in my eyes by proclaiming liberty, each to his neighbor, . . . but then you turned around and profaned my name when each of you took back his male and female slaves, whom you had set free according to their desire, and you brought them into subjection to be your slaves" (Jer. 34:15-16). Another thing that pleases God is this: "I desire steadfast love and not sacrifice, the knowledge of God, rather than burnt offerings" (Hos. 6:6).

Turning to God calls for both love and knowledge. But knowledge of God does not mean an intellectual grasp of the fact that God exists and an understanding of God's attributes. To know God means to do justice to the poor: "Your father. . . judged the cause of the poor and needy; then it was well. Is not this to know me? says the Lord" (Jer. 22:15-16).

According to the Hebrew way of thinking conversion meant separating oneself from evil and acting justly. But evil in this context is not something abstract or generic. The reference is rather to crimes, the oppression of the poor, the exploitation of the widow and the orphan.

As we continue our reading of the Bible, we see that the act of conversion is also an affirmation of life: "Come, let us *return* to the Lord. . . . After two days he will revive us; on the third day he will raise us up" (Hos. 6:1-2).

Even the wicked person who undergoes a real conversion will experience true life: "Though I say to the wicked, 'You shall surely die,' yet if he turns from his sin and does what is lawful and right, if the wicked . . . walks in the statutes of life, committing no iniquity, he shall surely live, he shall not die. None of the sins that he has committed shall be remembered against him; he has done what is lawful and right, he shall surely live" (Ezek. 33:14-16).

In the New Testament there are very few instances in which *metanoia* means simply remorse. In the majority of texts the meaning of *metanoia* is a radical change of outlook (accompanied, of course, by concrete actions). In its religious and ethical meaning the term is in the line of the Old Testament and Jewish concept of conversion.[3]

At the same time, however, the word in its New Testament usage conveys some ideas not found in the Old Testament. One of these is the pressing need of conversion to the kingdom of God, which is already at hand: "The time is fulfilled, and the kingdom of God is at hand; repent, and believe in the gospel" (Mark 1:15).

In the New Testament conversion occurs only once and is permanent.

Like *shub* in the prophets, *metanoia* in the New Testament implies a positive and real internal change that must give evidence of itself in all areas of life. The Pharisees and Sadducees believed that because they knew the Law and were descended from Abraham they had no need of *turning to God* or *being converted*. But John the Baptist tells them: "You brood of vipers! Who warned you to flee from the wrath to come? Bear fruit that befits repentance, and do not presume to say to yourselves, 'We have Abraham as our father' " (Matt. 3:7–9).

Chapter 3 of Luke's Gospel tells us clearly and unambiguously what kind of fruits must accompany conversion. When the people ask John the Baptist what they are to do, he answers them: "He who has two coats, let him share with him who has none; and he who has food, let him do likewise" (Luke 3:11).

Just actions are always linked to conversion. They are manifestations of the kingdom, to be done by individuals and groups in their own particular situations. Thus, when the tax collectors who served the Roman Empire asked John what fruits of conversion they in particular had to show, he answered: "Collect no more than is appointed you" (Luke 3:13). The soldiers present asked a similar question, and John answered that they must do violence to no one and not bear any false witness.

In summary: the act of conversion comprises two inseparable elements, a change of outlook and the bearing of the fruits proper to conversion.

Conversion is always accompanied by the acceptance of the

Good News: "Repent, and believe in the gospel." To "have faith" or to "believe" are terms that have a quite specific meaning. To believe means to believe that the kingdom of God is at hand and that the justice of God must be manifested and for all. Faith is effective when it produces the works of justice.

Conversion is an affirmation of human existence, since it is a response to God's call to life. It is not a simple change of mind but a complete re-creation of those who accept it. Paul says: "If any one is in Christ, he is a new creation; the old has passed away, behold, the new has come" (2 Cor. 5:17).

Conversion is a passage from death to life. The passage can be won only through obedience to the most important of all the commandments: love of neighbor. "We know that we have passed out of death into life, because we love the brethren. He who does not love remains in death" (1 John 3:14). Love of neighbor implies belief in God's word: "He who hears my word and believes him who sent me . . . has passed from death to life" (John 5:24).

There is no magic about a conversion. It demands a choice, and there can be no denying that a judgment of condemnation awaits those who do not choose to be converted, that is, to collaborate and share in the establishment of the kingdom of life here on earth by acting justly and promoting the welfare of the majority (Matt. 11:22; 12:41).

The Unconverted

Today there are many people who, like the Pharisees, believe that simply because they know the Church's dogmas and the books of the Bible or because they receive communion, they have a share in the kingdom of God. But they are wrong. Jesus himself says: "Not every one who says to me, 'Lord, Lord,' shall enter the kingdom of heaven, but he who does the will of my Father who is in heaven" (Matt. 7:21).

This is the stumbling block for many. They resemble the rich young man who thought he would inherit eternal life because he knew the Decalogue, but was unable to obey Jesus' call: "One thing you still lack. Sell all that you have and distribute to the poor . . ." (Luke 18:22).

Today we ask: How can those in command of oppressive re-

gimes participate in the Eucharist since all their actions are a
denial of the gospel of life? How can the name of Christian be
claimed by the stockholders in the great corporations or by those
who monopolize the means of production and exploit workers in
such deadly ways; or by those who talk of human rights but at
the same time approve shipments of military aid to dictatorial
regimes so that the latter may open the door to the multinational
corporations?

But the thing that is most incomprehensible is how there can
be bishops, archbishops, priests, pastors, and religious who give
communion to such individuals who are nothing but the personi-
fication of death. How is it possible at this juncture of history to
preach a dehistoricized and depoliticized gospel and, if that
weren't already too much, a gospel of condemnation, abnega-
tion, magic, and satanic dominion? Jesus said: "Not every one
who says to me, 'Lord, Lord,' shall enter the kingdom of
heaven."

Conversion as a Matter of Choice

The difficulty of conversion is a difficulty of choosing. A
choice must be made to enter into life and share in others' search
for life.

Inasmuch as conversion is a matter of choice, it entails conflict. When one possesses a certain socioeconomic position, a
break is inevitable if there is to be a conversion. Gustavo Gutiérrez says: "To wish to accomplish it [conversion] without conflict
is to deceive oneself and others."[4]

Almost all who have written on the subject of conversion are
in agreement on this point. It has been said that a conversion
must be radical to the point "of confronting death in order to
achieve a resurrection."[5] Jon Sobrino claims that the exhorta-
tion: "Repent, and believe in the gospel," has an element of
intimidation in it. "Now is the time to make a decision, and it
will entail a conversion, . . . a radical change in one's form of
existence."[6]

This inescapable break takes the form of a rejection of the
present, in which death is at work or, in other words, the oppression exercised by the socioeconomic conditions in which we are
caught. If conversion is what we say it is—a change of outlook

that impels us inexorably to hasten the process of liberation (so that the masses may have the right to life)—then conflict is inevitable. For conversion brings with it an identification of opposites and a definitive confrontation.

Conversion is a gift of God because it shows us the way and invites us to enter the world of freedom, the world of life. But at the same time conversion is a human task, because it demands of us an individual and collective commitment to the building of that world.

The kingdom of freedom of which I am speaking is meant to be a home for all the dishonored and humiliated people of the entire world. These are not few in number; they are rather the majority. This is why Jesus told his disciples on one occasion:

> You know that those who are supposed to rule over the Gentiles lord it over them, and their great men exercise authority over them. But it shall not be so among you; but whoever would be great among you must be your servant, and whoever would be first among you must be slave of all. For the Son of man also came not to be served but to serve, and to give his life as a ransom of many [Mark 10:42–45].

In the light of all that I have been saying, we have no choice but to say that conversion is a conversion to our neighbor—not to just any neighbor, however, but to this majority that has been deprived of its God-given right to enjoy life. In being thus converted to our neighbor we also turn to God, for it is only if we love our neighbor that we can see God (1 John 4:12).

In order to drive this point home I quote these words of Gustavo Gutiérrez: "Conversion means a radical transformation of ourselves; it means thinking, feeling, and living as Christ— present in exploited and alienated man. To be converted means to commit oneself to the process of the liberation of the poor and the oppressed, to commit oneself lucidly, realistically, and concretely."[7]

Such a lucid, realistic, and concrete commitment means that the following of Christ calls logically for organization, strategy, and the tactical means that may be required for making the kingdom of God a reality. But that is another subject.

NOTES

1. Rudolf Schnackenburg, *Christian Existence in the New Testament,* trans. F. Wieck (Notre Dame, Ind.: University of Notre Dame Press, 1968), 1:36.
2. See J. Behm and E. Würthwein, "noeō," TDNT, 4:980.
3. Ibid., 4:999.
4. Gustavo Gutiérrez, *A Theology of Liberation,* trans. Sister Caridad Inda and John Eagleson (Maryknoll, N.Y.: Orbis Books, 1973), p. 205.
5. V. Cosmao, "De una práctica del desarrollo a una teología de la conversión," in E. Ruiz Maldonado, ed., *Liberación y Cautiverio: Encuentro Latinoamericano de Teología* (Mexico City, 1975), p. 305.
6. Jon Sobrino, *Christology at the Crossroads: A Latin American Approach,* trans. John Drury (Maryknoll, N.Y.: Orbis Books, 1978), p. 56.
7. Gutiérrez, *A Theology of Liberation,* p. 205.

CONCLUSION

BREAKING THE OPPRESSION/LIBERATION CYCLE

We have seen that the Bible records frequent experiences of oppression and subsequent liberation. There is, however, no definitive liberation. Liberation is a process; as Leonardo Boff says, it "is a task that must continually be accomplished anew," because "liberation does not yet mean liberty."[1]

It is a fact, nonetheless, that in the new covenant hopes become deeper and closer to fulfillment because of the supreme self-revelation of God in human form. The historical career of Jesus makes possible an indissoluble union of God and humanity without any loss of identity on either side. God's reign here on earth has begun. Through Jesus of Nazareth the God of the Hebrews is now "in ontological solidarity" with all the oppressed of our human history, and unqualified liberation will be universal and not restricted to the narrow world of the Jews.[2]

The resurrection of Jesus has put an end to the cycle of oppression–liberation–oppression–liberation: Through the resurrection "the utopian truth of the kingdom becomes a reality here and now; it becomes an event which gives assurance that the

83

process of liberation will not remain an endless cycle of oppression and liberation but will lead to a complete and limitless liberation."[3]

For the oppressed this unqualified liberation, which has begun in the praxis and victory of the Suffering Servant, Jesus Christ, who identifies himself with the entire race, is especially urgent in the sociopolitical field, but it is also open to an *eschaton* that transcends political liberation and includes "liberation from that which vitiates all human projects (i.e., sin), as well as the conquest of death."[4]

My express intention in reading the Bible has been to discover the Christian meaning of our Latin American history. The oppressive situation in the countries around us, the oppression weighing on the masses, but also the signs of resistance and liberation that are to be seen, all oblige us at every moment to inquire of the biblical text how we are to live the faith here and now.

Oppression in Latin America is certainly brutal and cruel, but for that very reason the struggle of the people is constantly intensifying. And Christians, summoned by their faith, are dedicating themselves to the building of the kingdom of God; they are supported by the firm hope that they will be able to say, with John the Apostle, "Then I saw a new heaven and a new earth" (Rev. 21:1).

NOTES

1. Leonardo Boff, *Teología desde el Cautiverio* (Bogotá: Indo-American Press Service, 1975), p. 81.
2. Ibid., p. 164.
3. Ibid., p. 169.
4. Ibid.

Scriptural Index

NEW TESTAMENT